high heels

FASHION   FEMININITY   SEDUCTION

EDITED BY IVAN VARTANIAN

WITH CONTRIBUTIONS BY

JAMES CRUMP

VALERIE STEELE

TIM BLANKS

PHILIP DELAMORE

STELLA BRUZZI

INTERVIEWS WITH

MANOLO BLAHNÍK,

NICHOLAS KIRKWOOD & CHARLOTTE OLYMPIA

Thames & Hudson

Maison Martin Margiela, Autumn/Winter 2009.
Photograph © Julien Oppenheim. Courtesy
Maison Martin Margiela (NEUF SAS).

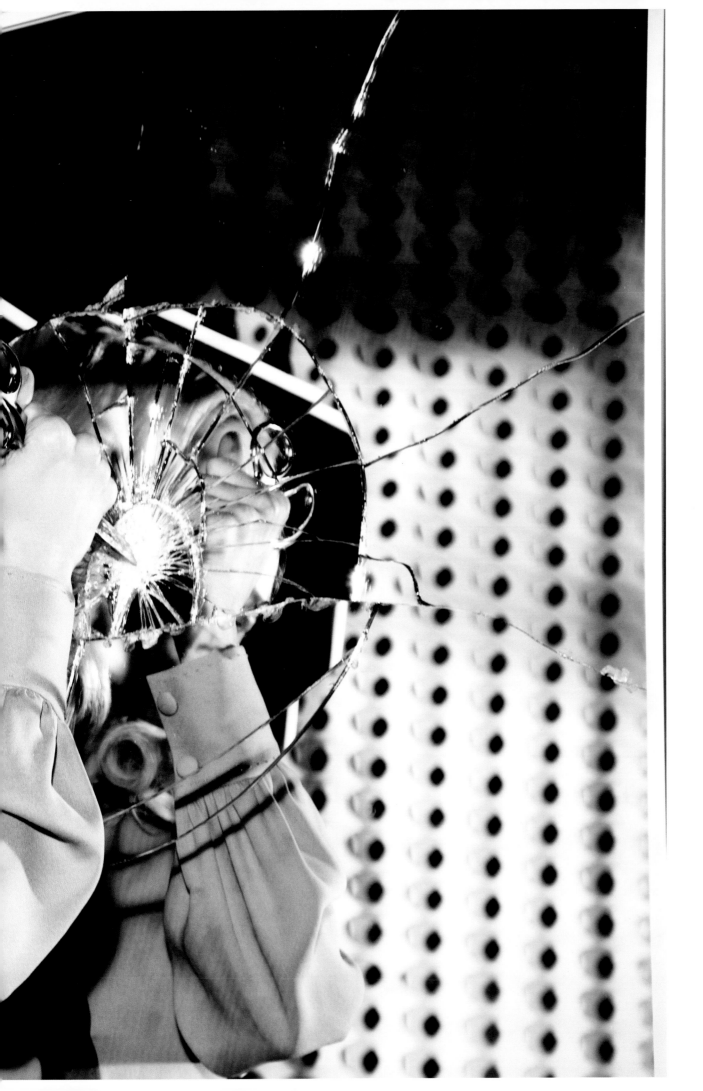

11

Introduction:

Nude in Heels, or, A Fetish for Photography

by Ivan Vartanian

A high heel not only transforms the silhouette of a foot and extends the line of the leg, it functions as a type of prosthetic to hobble the wearer to some degree. In doing so, its ulterior (and truer) function takes effect, which is to make the wearer a spectacle. The photograph, in its hungry search for well-delineated negative space or graphic and tonal relationships in its composition, also morphs the form of its subjects. On this point, the two—the high heel and the photograph—have a sort of intimate collusion, a perfect partnership acting to transform the body in order to appease a fetish for strong images. It seems only natural that something so unnatural as the high-heeled shoe—a symbol of power and strength in itself—should be so well suited to the photographic process of framing and compositional organization. Likewise, the photograph is in symbiosis with the high heel; a medium that remains distinct from the other visual arts—with its own language and syntax—as, say, architecture. A photograph, in directing the movement of the eye to flick from point to directed point, arrests our attention on its very surface. It is simultaneously a window onto reality as well as an illusion, a product of its own surfaceness. This dualism and the effect it has on viewers leads us to continually question the photographic truth of an image—a tension that is on par with the power of a fetish object. In this way, dealing with the high heel and the photograph at the same time is like the overlay of one lens on top of another. In other words, the way in which we relate to photography has a fetishistic charge.

While the term fetish now generally connotes something dealing with sex, the word in its original usage meant an object believed to have supernatural power, particularly a man-made object believed to possess power over others. The high heel is a steadfast locus for representing femininity, mature sexuality, fashion, and power—all of which are social constructs. Photographs from the archives of the Kinsey Institute show shoe fetishism (pages 18–19) as an extension of the wearer's dominance, as though the heel itself attributes her with special power along with the disciplinary riding crop the mistress holds. In recent years, in particular, as the high-heeled shoe (and other accessories) has taken on signifiers such as fashionability, status, and wealth, the heel's very form has gone through an intense growth spurt. An extremely long heel set against an acute pitch of the arch is a commonplace accoutrement for the well-shod; a hidden platform under the ball of the foot can further lift the wearer off the ground and allow for an even lengthier heel (pages 107–108, 175–178). Extremity, intense embellishment, and idolatry of the high heel have transformed it from a skinny spike into a heavily garnished thing in itself, with an air of architecture (pages 65–67), retaining its shape regardless of whether it holds a wearer's foot or not. In this process, the appeal of the

Miles Aldridge, Christian Louboutin's Lady Lynch shoe, shot for the *New Yorker*, 2011.

high heel resembles the commodity fetishism that Marx explains in *Das Kapital*, wherein social relationships are co-opted by the relationship of commodities. In this case, we are dealing with a luxurious item but it remains a manufactured and branded commodity nonetheless. The reshaping and remodeling of the heel has been carried out extensively. This trend toward extreme heels—increasing height—is a part of fashion oneupmanship. In a recent collection, DSquared created a curved heel that closely resembled a spinal column comprised of individually rendered vertebrae. Feats of engineering and design acumen set the foot on a cantilevered shoe that is heelless, giving the impression of the wearer floating on air, as with the heel designed by Noritaka Tatehana (page 175). Or the shape of the foot is entirely recast, as was done by Alexander McQueen with his iconic Armadillo Shoes of 2010 (page 177). For the Chanel Cruise collection in 2009, a downward-pointing gun served as the heel for a shoe that was labeled The Killer. The resemblance of fashion shoots to visions of violence was certainly not uncommon in the 1970s (pages 34–35, 44–45) and has since transformed into a leitmotif of sorts, with models transfixed like a corpse (page 70–71) or put in more comical but no less threatening predicaments (page 154–155). There can be indeed something harsh about how a photograph renders its subject if we take it to be anything more than an instantaneous representation. The photograph, in

its cropping and framing, can disassemble the subject's form, much like an illusionist performing a magic trick on stage with his assistant. In Antonio Lopez's Instamatics his photographs of a woman's form are organized into a grid format (pages 36, 37, 41). In this manner, the photographer recreates the line of sight of the Instamatic, which sees the form in sections with its pinpoint gaze of the lens. In assembling the frames in this way, the body is reassembled as the camera sees the form, unnaturally reformatting the proportions of the body as segments.

Marilyn Minter's iconic *Green Pink Caviar* (2009) video shot in high definition with a macro lens blurs the boundary between fine art and commercial art. In her images of heels included here (pages 124–129), there is a decidedly *un*beautiful aspect intermixed with the luxury items as the model's feet seem to wade through muck and grime. The high definition of the image is part and parcel of its erotic charge. In its version of perfection, it lifts its subject from the mundane into the realm of photographic reality. Elsewhere, the use of high speed photography in tight closeups for beauty photography re-renders the model's face as a product with technically precise control of lighting. The resulting quality is surreal on one hand (page 68–69) and abstract on another (page 75).

In this heightened attention to the heel, there is an element of erotic fetishism, of course, but as in Robert Mapplethorpe's portrait of *Melody's Shoe* (pages 48–49), the Dionysian impulse

Bela Borsodi, from the series "Skin Flicker," shot for S Magazine, 2010.

balanced with the neoclassical confiscates an overt sexualization, making the image and the heel more about the identity of the wearer—even though we only see her extremity. Elsewhere in Mapplethorpe's oeuvre, as in his notorious *X Portfolio*, the artist presents portraits of his sitters that would otherwise have an overt sexual charge but this is held at bay by a more powerful charge of beauty—the erotic charge being sublimated into the pleasure of looking at the photograph. More to the point, Mapplethorpe had an extraordinary gift of reducing the elements of his photographs to such a taut minimum that the content was transformed into something larger and more potent than the physicality of the object being photographed. Similarly, Maison Martin Margiela's glass slipper shot with a low-key photographic approach (pages 8–9) reinterprets Cinderella's slipper as a high-heeled shoe, though there is no explicit definition of the shoe as such provided by the brand. But if Cinderella's tale were to be written nowadays, she would most certainly have worn a high-heeled shoe with an acute pitch.

An element of danger and crime—or transgression at least—is a natural fit for the high heel and its association with the *femme fatale*. She is a seductress who brings destruction—and excitement—to the man with whom she becomes involved. She is beautiful and dangerous at the same time. Ellen von Unwerth poses a model before a cracked mirror with eyes glaring back at the camera, a pair of cutting shears in hand (pages 10–11). This shot references the 1978 film *Eyes of Laura Mars*, starring Faye Dunaway as a high fashion photographer in New York. Mars has visions of violent murders as seen through the eyes of a killer. "When it happens, I can't see what's in front of me. What I see is *that*," she says, pointing to a video monitor hooked into a camera. She continues, "Think of that camera as the eyes of a killer." In the film, a detective, played by Tommy Lee Jones, shows Mars black-and-white photographs of crime scenes, positioning them directly beside her color fashion photographs, and says, "These are police photographs. They are strictly our own material and were never published anywhere at all. So the question is very

simple." Dunaway's character articulates the rest, "Why are my photographs so much like yours?"

This scene, where two different types of photography are compared side-by-side readily evokes a body of work called *Evidence*, published in 1977 by Larry Sultan in collaboration with artist Mike Mandel. The photographs in *Evidence* were assembled from the files of government agencies, corporations, and research facilities. Images such as graphic documentation—stripped of so-called artifice—were re-contextualized by Sultan and Mandel in a sequence that was devoid of any information. As a result, the images, took on a new, relational meaning and function through their new context, edit, and sequence—even though that meaning and intent is never explicitly stated anywhere. The project of that endeavor was a meditation on how a viewer cannot resist assigning value and meaning as a direct outcome of sequence and editing. The sense of sight has an altering effect, and the assembly of images has a transformative effect, giving the images a different function and form that is—at

times—totally devoid of the original meaning or purpose. Laura Mars, as a photographer who has visions of things that aren't before her, sums up the work of photographers, who labor to see as the camera sees or to make the camera see as they do.

In Lise Sarfati's work (pages 132–135) from the series "Austin, Texas," the interaction between photography—creating images within the language of strict reportage—and the women who take center focus has been a fascinating component throughout Sarfati's career. In this photographer's patient looking, the photograph is not a means of probing or exposure, freezing her subjects in a moment to reveal something hidden. The slowness and deliberation of her images underscore how her subjects seem to be a part of the process, building the image in conjunction with Sarfati. Fashion in this context is about how the items of clothing project the personality of the wearer and are on a par with gesture and expression in providing a visual means of introspection and investigation. In another sense, clothing underscores the performative aspect of identity. The eventlessness of her

Opposite: Unknown photographer, 1944. This page: Unknown photographer, 1937–1941. Both images courtesy the archives of The Kinsey Institute for Research in Sex, Gender, and Reproduction. Following spread: Miles Aldridge, *Dance Study, Paradis*, 2008.

images still has a tenor of drama, as her subjects become spectacles, not of the exotic but of readable and unreadable signifiers that culminate in a suggestion (as opposed to a statement). For Sarfati, the photographer can only ever suggest a possible understanding of her subject.

The two compositions by Larry Sultan included in this book are from his series "The Valley" (pages 136–139). The series addresses the appropriation of middle-class homes for use as pornographic film locales. When Sultan made his images, there was an amplified sense of dislocation between the action and the setting that at the same time underscores the indeterminate (and perhaps non-existent) distinction between truth and fiction, between the portrayal of sex and the reality of domesticity. Performer Sharon Wild sits at the edge of a bed in disarray (pages 138–139) looking contemplative and even bored, an expression which is wholly appropriate for such a mundane environment. In a similar way, Jeff Burton's *Untitled #36* composition set on a Hollywood poolside blurs the line between art, porn,

and fashion (pages 164–165). And that happily uneasy balance underscores an inherent tension in photography to simultaneously serve as illustration, as something beyond language, and as an experience in itself.

In the 1983 film *Videodrome* by David Cronenberg, an executive of a small cable station starts having hallucinations of violent scenes, not unlike Laura Mars. In search for answers and to delve further into the world of Videodrome, Max Renn, the executive played by James Woods, searches out the mysterious Professor Brian O'Blivion, who in a videotaped monologue states his philosophy: "The television screen has become the retina of the mind's eye. Therefore, the television screen is part of the physical structure of the brain. Therefore, whatever appears on the television screen emerges as raw experience for those who watch it. Therefore, television is reality. And reality is less than television." The act of seeing a broadcast image is realer than the experience of the temporal world; the television, or the photograph, trumps actual experience. The effect

This page: Guy Aroch, 2006, "Rejuvenation," for *ELLE France*.
Opposite: Tommy Ton, YSL, Autumn/Winter 2009 New York Fashion Week.

of Videodrome is to morph the body into a videocassette player (as a form of mind control), converting people into automatons, whose appendages are part machine or weapon. The sculptor Allen Jones, in his 1969 artworks, contorted the female form into the shape of furniture, such as tables, chairs, and a chest of drawers (page 120). His mannequin sculptures wore knee-length high-heeled boots, corsets as well as other items typical of bondage.

The high heel transforms the body—adding height and thereby changing the line of sight and perspective. The small change in position is on par with the distance between the viewfinder and the lens; the eye and the lens are not in the same position and the apparatus and the eye see two different things; the latter being quickly over-written by the photograph that remains. In this sense, the camera is a prosthetic eye, doing the seeing for us, supplying us with a photographic reality. Allen's sculpture of the front part of a woman's torso is both a mold and armor (page 121). A corset made by Mr Pearl is not unlike a harness or an appendage to the body (pages 82–83). The high heel itself

is like body armor or a prosthesis but it is also restrictive, blurring the distinction between what is a device for self-protection versus constriction—and in many ways these qualities are conflated. These tropes of bondage have had their sartorial lexicon wholly appropriated by contemporary fashion (pages 86–89). Fashion images—by tapping into something more primal and real—also create such a photographic reality. Despite their set-up-ness and projection of fantasy, there is a sexual realness in these fashion images enabled by photography as a function of some fantasy. The photographs are sexual artifacts, much like how the high heel can be a fetish object.

The prosthetic artificiality of the heel is what gives it its power. Indeed, prostheses gave Aimee Mullins "super powers," as she describes in her TED talk of 2009. Born without fibulae in both legs, she wears prosthetics below the knee. But when wearing feather-light carbon-fiber prostheses modeled on the appendages of a cheetah, she set world records for the 100 meters, 200 meters and long jump. She appears as a cheetah in Matthew Barney's *Cremaster 3* (pages 98–99) and also wears

clear transparent legs that have a heel built in (page 131). (Barney, good sport, wears a pair of mid-height heels, too.)

In this selection and sequence of images of high heels, rather than being a "Where's Waldo" process of finding the high heel in each image, I wanted to reach for an image of femininity that is complicated and intriguing and make this book less of a catalog of brand name heel designs and more of a meditation on what the high heel has come to mean in fashion and in our collective ideas about body form. Apart from fashion, this book is also about seduction and femininity and how these themes are entwined with reading photography. The fleshed-out sequence presents the material as one integrated photobook, rather than treating the images as mere illustrations. To that end, there may be some unexpected inclusions within the edit that, in turn, open up the visual language of the project. For example, a close-up of a flower's reproductive parts by Nobuyoshi Araki (page 55) is reminiscent of Georgia O'Keeffe's paintings and also plugs into the visual process of identifying forms and visual allusion. In a similar way, the high heel is a stand-in for something else—a whole array of interpretations, symbols, and meanings.

Fashion's ability to take such references and divorce them of their original meaning is probably its greatest potential, and not unlike uniforms that give their wearers their station, fashion consumes all of these references and discharges something that has made artificiality and extremity a self-serving norm. Photography, on the other hand, looks to organize and make sense of disparate elements, making fashion photography serve as two rails of a ladder—it is both an image of fashion and it is fashion itself. But what it hunts for is something that has an edge to it; something that gives a shock to its viewer. In *Videodrome*, just before Max Renn begins his descent into violent hallucinations, he says, "I am looking for something that will break through. Something *tough*."

Guy Bourdin, shot for *Vogue Paris*, 1977.
Following spread: Unpublished image, circa 1965.

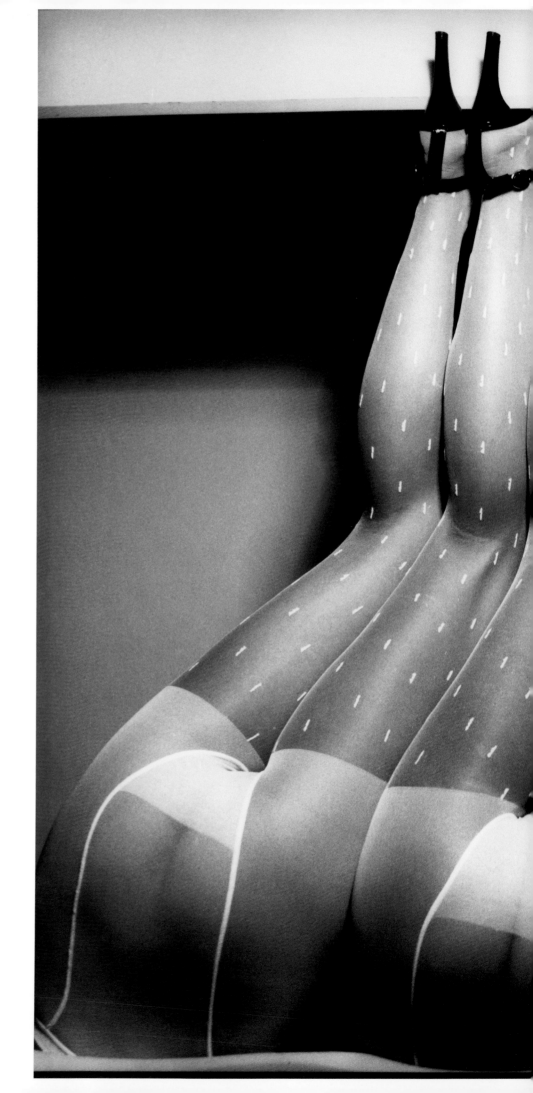

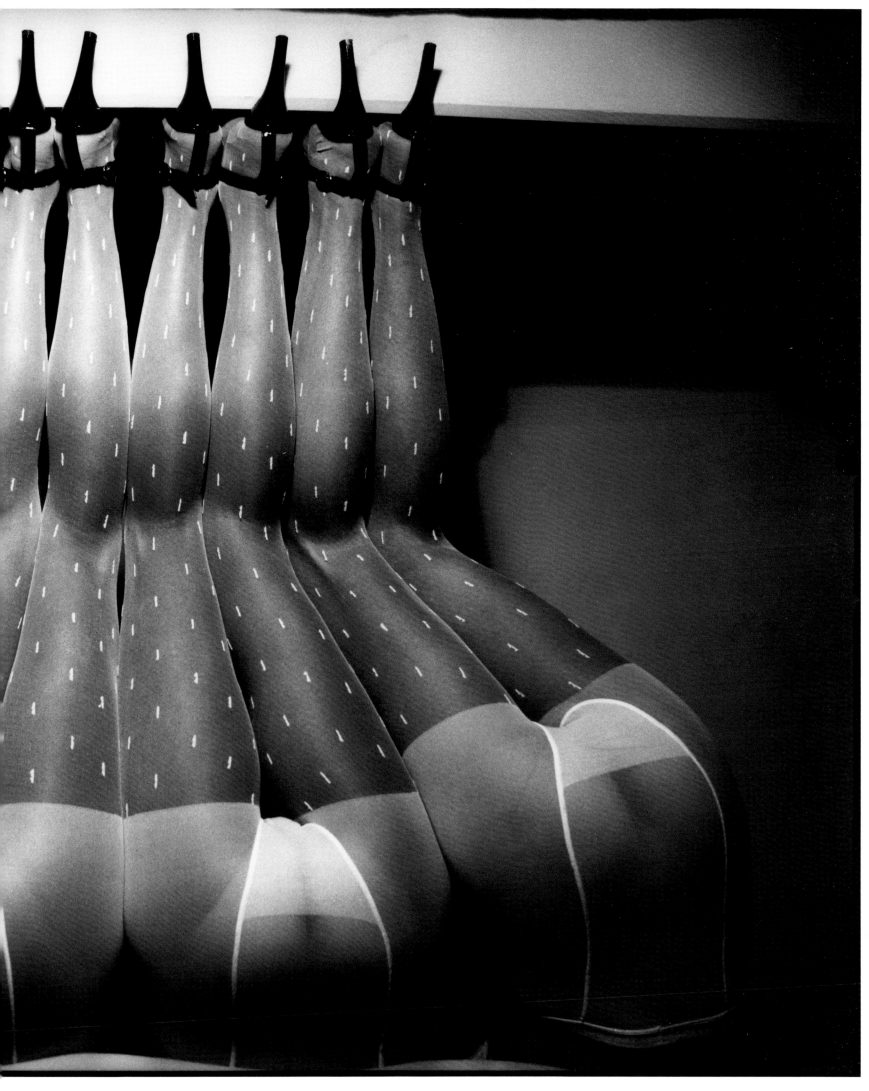

Guy Bourdin, shot for Charles Jourdan, 1977.

This spread: Guy Bourdin. This page, above: shot for *Vogue Paris*, 1979. This page, below: shot for Charles Jourdan, 1975. Opposite, above: shot for Roland Pierre, 1983. Opposite, below: shot for Charles Jourdan, 1978.

Shoot to Thrill: Fetishism and Fashion Photography in the 1970s

by James Crump

Among the least known but remarkably potent time capsules of the 1970s is the trove of Instamatic photographs left behind by artist and fashion illustrator, Antonio Lopez. In literally thousands of images, populated by vibrant and beautiful young people—designers, artists, writers, models, actors, impresarios and other hangers on—it is nearly possible to breathe in the air of this heady, decadent decade, now a bygone era. Most arresting about many of these often highly staged and directed snapshots is a lingering essence of *jouissance*, the palpable residue of after sex wafting from these Pop-colored morsels and a very definite sense that in pre-AIDS Paris and New York these people were having one hell of a good time.

There was a lot of fucking going on, but that's not exactly the point of Antonio's images in contrast, say, to Robert Mapplethorpe's contemporaneous black-and-white hard-core pictures of sex. Antonio's Instamatic pictures likewise lack much of the severity, the "Germanic perfectionism" characterizing the stream of fashion photographs of this period in which they circulated—they

rather possess a poignant naturalism of real people flourishing in a social matrix of endless possibilities, both sexual and professional, as if gender stereotypes and difference never existed, where "straight" and "gay" held little currency en lieu of a decidedly ambisexual aesthetic. It all seemed so simple then.[1]

Despite their set-up-ness, the Instamatic pictures suggest Antonio was discovering for himself a new kind of photographic reality that transcended both the merely pornographic and the popular images circulating in the glossy magazines. The Instamatics are tinged with personal fantasy and voyeuristic potential, as Antonio incites his subjects to play along in completing the sequence of his erotic narratives, however kinky or perverse. As sexual artifacts, these pictures leave behind a distinctly visceral trace of what it was like, that titillating sensation of one having been there. The rapport Antonio shared with his subjects, both male and female, is strikingly evident. Young women on the cusp of being discovered—Jerry Hall (page 40), Jessica Lange and Tina Chow, for instance, and many lesser

known beauties—shamelessly frolic, sometimes in bathtubs filled with bubbly blue dye or are shown bound and gagged with rubber hose and ribbon or pulling at their panties and tube tops. The men in these images, too, are equally natural in their exhibitionism; they don toy space helmets or playfully pull their cocks through zippered flies. One man mocks phone sex, but evidently he feels free enough in the photographer's presence to ejaculate for the camera.[2]

Andy Warhol was most successful in branding the instantaneous snapshot, notwithstanding its simultaneous popularity among many other great visual artists. Yet, even Warhol's Polaroids depicting explicit sex seem clinical in contrast to Antonio's pictures; they lack the raw, primal, reality effect of the Instamatics to which fashion photography begins to aspire in this period; an evolution toward a permanent sea change in the fashion image brought forward most notably in photographs by Helmut Newton, Guy Bourdin and Chris von Wangenheim. With Antonio, all three artists presaged a dawning image machine that continues to

exploit our darkest fantasies, however mainstream and homogenous they may seem, or rather have been rendered today with the prevalence of social media and "reality" programming. The predictable provocations of Terry Richardson, for example, or the mannered perversions of Mert and Marcus, not to mention the plethora of minimalist, and sterilely serviceable internet porn, all rather pale in comparison to the work of these precursors who collectively mark the fetish power of fashion photography that is now a permanent and ubiquitous condition of advertising and popular media; art, film, gaming and video.

"The violence is in the culture so why shouldn't it be in our pictures," commented Chris von Wangenheim in a 1977 *Time* article addressing "brutality chic" in advertising and the prevalence of fashion images showing women bound, gagged, beaten or enduring other brutal acts.[3] Von Wangenheim understood how to ratchet up an ambience of danger and aggression in his pictures. In images like *Woman Smashing a TV Set*, the photographer demonstrates his savvy in unleashing sexually loaded

symbols, in this instance representing the glass shards of the television screen as so many rough-cut diamonds on which his model forcefully grinds her high heels. Art directors and fashion critics at the time were struggling with how to describe what for von Wangenheim was merely "elegant sensuality and sexuality."[4] More challenging images show his reverence in exploring taboo subjects; the terms of "anti-fashion" surfacing in photography in the 1970s that mirrored a broader cultural plunge into decadence and self indulgence.[5]

Like the surrealists, especially artist Hans Bellmer, von Wangenheim seems equally obsessed with the uncanny, transmogrified image of the female body. In his *Girl Standing on Her Head*, for example, the photographer turns his model's arms into legs, reordering her high heels and pubis to upper body positions. Male domination, rape, and violence against women were also surrealist subtexts. Von Wangenheim's *Tattooed Girl* features a high-heel-clad model that, in addition to receiving a tattoo, seems also to be penetrated from behind. Whether the act is consensual

remains ambiguous; von Wangenheim shows the tattoo artist jubilantly pointing his index finger; a doubting Thomas, inspecting his design as if it were the very wounds of Christ.

In a forthcoming monograph of his Instamatic pictures, Antonio's shared obsession with high heels is readily apparent.[6] He plays with these objects as both sex toys and weapons for penetration, but in contrast to von Wangenheim, the Instamatics are chiefly about self-willed pleasure in submission and autoeroticism. One series, for example, features a nude male sprawling on a set of stairs as a female subject uses her heels to explore and penetrate his sculpted behind. In this grid of six Instamatics, Antonio humorously juxtaposes the probing heel with an equal number of coquettish close-ups that feature a young woman's piercing green eyes—as if to suggest the attainable girl next door is inviting the viewer to take part in the action. As Alicia Drake has pointed out in her indispensable study of Paris fashion in the 1970s, "Newton's and Bourdin's stylized images were heterosexual and born of a pre-war generation."[7] For Antonio, who on occasion did enjoy sex

with women, the new wave of inspiration in fashion was a post-modern amalgam crossing gay culture with a diverse urban street aesthetic and the nascent punk and S&M scenes; a seamy, some-times camp, admixture that had a powerful effect on the eventual waning of couture and the increasing popularity of *prêt-a-porter*. With obvious kinship to Mapplethorpe's fetish image, *Melody's Shoe*—a still life study of a dominatrix's patent leather pump—Antonio created a series of flaming high heel sculptures that he later meticulously photographed in sequence. High heels for Antonio were obviously charged, seductive objects, perhaps never more so than in the series of Instamatic pictures he made of a hunky, tanned young man who writhes poolside, wearing nothing more than a pair of red leather heels and a thong supporting his makeshift pony's tail. Today, we expect such fare from the likes of Juergen Teller or David LaChapelle. Antonio's pictures were made to share with his inner circle of friends, but they say much about the currents in photography—the subversive and countercultural attitudes of this time.

Between 1971 and 1972 in Paris and later in New York, Antonio's influence was profound. According to Anna Piaggi, he "was bringing the ethnic new culture" to bear on fashion, its young designers, their even younger models, and the street chic then gaining ground.[8] With Karl Lagerfeld, Antonio was helping free the fashion image from the postwar shackles of European tradition, experimenting with high and low forms, and intuiting the benefits of chance, spontaneity and rapid-fire execution in his work. Like Bourdin and Warhol, both of whom used Polaroid cameras, Antonio recognized the gritty, low-fi seduction of the instantaneous plastic coated image—fetish objects unto them-selves—containing both strangely saturated and muted colors and featuring super smooth surfaces that sometimes effected the look of metal or glass.

Known for his notorious work for Paris *Vogue* in the 1970s, Guy Bourdin, more obviously than Antonio, hastened our fetish obsession with fashion photography, commingling images of suicidal or disembodied women, masturbation and high heels

into unsettling confections of supersaturated color with endless narrative potential. Like Antonio, Bourdin reveled in the disco era exhibitionism of Paris and New York, but the content of his photographs is more closely aligned with von Wangenheim and Newton, all three of whom traded on allusions to violence and sadomasochism, the "porno chic" underscored by Newton's 1976 book, *White Women*.

Among Bourdin's most beguiling images were those produced for Charles Jourdan shoes for whom, for twenty-two years, the photographer worked. In one particularly iconic image, featuring a maid and her *maîtresse de la maison*, dominance and submission are prominently on display. Shot in Karl Lagerfeld's Rue de l'Université apartment, a mistress reclines on a draped sofa, wearing a black negligee, as her maid kneels before her, fastening the metallic strap of the woman's stiletto heel. The image is suffused with erotic possibility; indeed, it begs viewers to fill in the voids of this broken narrative and what might or might not transpire; bondage and lesbian sex. Bourdin started out as

a painter, and in preparation for this composition he produced a drawing that today amplifies the artist's proclivities, physically played out on set with his models and studio assistants. In the drawing, two maids are shown with their mistress—the setting for a more complex *ménage à trois*—one maid whispering into her ear while the other maid kneels, seeming to kiss the woman's feet. Numerous contact sheets left behind from this shoot witness Bourdin's perfectionism, his obsession to find the ideal tension between master and slave, top and bottom. Such highly directed and staged photographic tableaux are the predominant mainstays of the contemporary art market today, which Bourdin's work foreshadowed by at least a quarter century.

Bourdin's reputation notwithstanding, Helmut Newton comes out ahead in this fetishistic continuum for the sweeping effect his work has had on fashion photography in particular and popular culture more generally. Few, if any, of the leading fashion photographers today could say with any truthfulness that Newton was *not* an important influence on their respective careers. Newton's

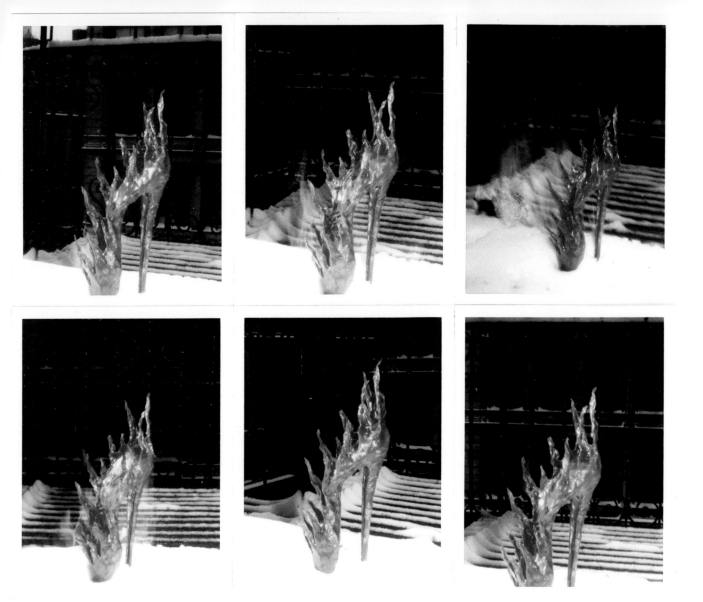

prominence began much earlier, but certainly his more recent broad popularity can be attributed to the release of his giant tome, *Sumo*, in 2000 and a succession of exhibitions featuring his work. Today, a relatively broad market exists for the collective surplus of Newton's expensive, high-end vintage photographs, trade books and other licensed products that have nearly established this once outré photographer as a household name.

"When I see a woman," Newton once declared, "I always look immediately at her shoes and hope they're high because high heels make a woman look sexy and dangerous."[9] If Bourdin's photographs were crueler, as Newton believed them to be, his own pictures hew closest to heterosexual fantasy and desire. He constantly placed a premium on menacing, voluptuous models, often nude except for high heels in both recognizably posh and uncanny pedestrian settings. Newton was a master of the *mise-en-scène* using provocative props—video cameras and monitors, saddlery, guns and robotics. In one memorable portfolio series for *Vogue* from 1995, featuring model Nadja Auermann, he

even used prostheses to remarkable effect. In the series, High and Mighty, Auermann is first shown depicted in a wheelchair wearing Chanel stiletto slingbacks. In subsequent pictures she walks with metal crutches, and later her maimed leg is supported by a stainless steel armature, thus transforming her into one of the photographer's signature black widows; wearing black ankle-wrapped ribbon stilettos, Auermann is a visual analogue to the character Gabrielle in J.G. Ballard's 1973 novel, *Crash*.

The democratization of technology has put cell phone cameras in all of our pockets, doing what the Kodak Instamatic and Polaroid cameras did in the 1970s. They fostered an obsessive desire for faster and faster means for instant, tactile gratification that today, more than ever, we demand in our daily consumption of images. The hyper-mediated photograph through which we consume fashion in the twenty-first century, however, seems bereft of the voyeuristic thrill so emblematic of Antonio's privately distributed pictures as well as the magazine work done for hire by Newton, Bourdin and von Wangenheim. As Luc Sante has

recently described today's consumer of literary fiction, "readers go for data, preferably without having to chop their way through idiosyncrasies such as style. For all we know, the pursuit of data will soon enough be free of the encumbrance and ambiguity of words."[10] Likewise, in our late capitalist society—when everything is monetized and everything is for sale—contemporary fashion photography is increasingly derivative and homogenous, given over to a similar function of data dissemination, where the projection of sexual fantasy and desire are more often displaced by the extremes of information that fashion images are now assigned to convey in the blur of constant visual overload and saturation. The present transition taking place before us, from traditional print media to digital viewing platforms serves only to compound and hasten this predicament. Antonio, von Wangenheim, Bourdin and Newton are more than instructive in this regard. In contrast to today's fashion photographers, their work collectively underscores just how much has changed in four decades, and how very different our experiences with fashion images are today.

1. Philippe Garner, quoted in Nancy Hall-Duncan, *The History of Fashion Photography*, New York: Alpine Book Company, 1979, p. 209.
2. A large number of these images are reproduced in *Antonio Lopez: Instamatics*, Santa Fe: Twin Palms Publishers, forthcoming 2011.
3. Chris von Wangenheim, *Time*, vol. 109, 1977, p. 516.
4. Chris von Wangenheim, quoted in Laurence Lotner, "Eyes of the '70s," in *Art Direction: The Magazine of Visual Communication*, December, 1975, p. 62.
5. See Valerie Steele's article, "Anti-Fashion: The 1970s", in *Fashion Theory*, vol. 1, no. 3, 1997, pp. 279–95.
6. Op. cit., note 2.
7. Alicia Drake, *The Beautiful Fall: Fashion, Genius, and Glorious Excess in 1970s Paris*, Boston and New York: Little, Brown and Co., 2007, p. 248.
8. Ibid., p. 128.
9. Helmut Newton, quoted in American *Vogue*, February, 1995, p. 230. Reprinted in Helmut Newton, *Pages from the Glossies*, New York and Zurich: Scalo Verlag, p. 511.
10. Luc Sante, "The Quick-Change Artist: The Miscellaneous Prose of Novelist, Memoirist, Critic, and First-Class Noticer Geoff Dyer," in *Bookforum*, Apr/May 2011, p. 14.

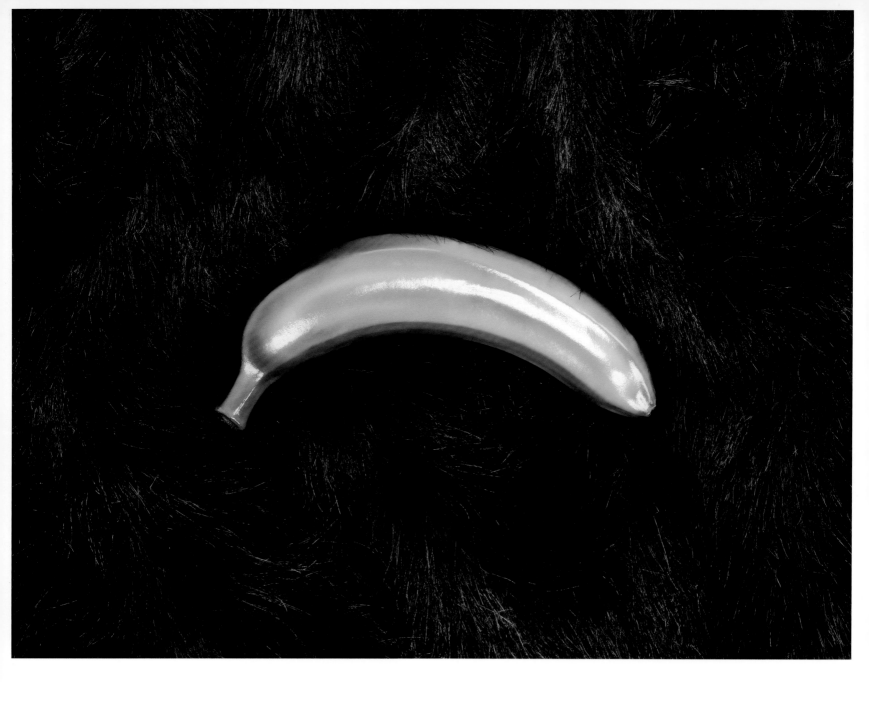

This spread: Aorta. Opposite: *Untitled*, 2007. This page: *Untitled*, shot for *125 Magazine*, 2009. Styling by Sally O'Sullivan, set design by Johan Svenson.

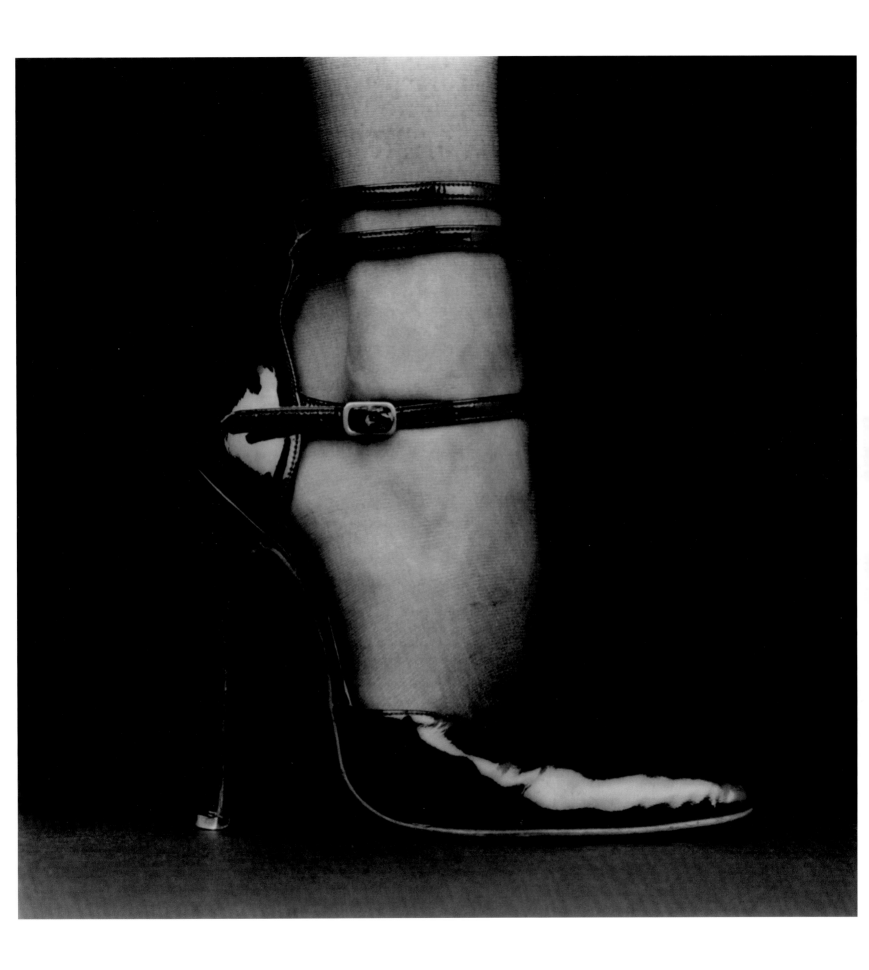

Sean and Seng, shot for *Numéro*, 2011.

Opposite: Mari Sarai, *Samantha Ma* from the series "Naked," 2010. Courtesy the artist and Angle Management. This page, above: Nobuyoshi Araki, *67 Shooting Back*, 2007. This page, below: Nobuyoshi Araki, *Hana Jinsei*, 2002. Both images courtesy Taka Ishii Gallery.

In Conversation: Valerie Steele

What did the high heel signify in the past, and what do you think it signifies now?

The meaning of any particular item of clothing, such as a high heel shoe, is not inherent in the object itself. It's entirely something that's constructed by people in the society around it. So in the past, high heel shoes carried very clear associations of elevated status and were initially worn by men as well as women. By the middle of the eighteenth century, however, they'd acquired to a considerable extent their contemporary meaning, which is primarily a sign of erotic femininity and, to some extent, simply femininity in general. Years ago, when I was traveling in the People's Republic of China, I saw a men's room sign that was a top hat and cane. The women's room sign was a pair of high heels. Obviously this had come from abroad. This was back in the 1970s when there weren't worn China. Nonetheless, this codification was already recognized as a sign of gender differentiation.

Why do you think women wear high heels?

That's a question with as many different answers as there are women. But essentially, elements that seem to be particularly common are women's perception of high heels as something feminine and sexy and they know that many men respond with an almost Pavlovian fervor to the sight of high heels. There may be a number of other more specific issues, such as the season's fashion or the wearer's height. As psychiatrists would say, it's overdetermined. Two things have been happening in the last ten years. One—especially in the last five years—heels have gotten higher and higher; platform shoes with a high platform and a very high narrow heel. Two: heels seem to have become the default high fashion shoe. Even though shoe companies and fashion magazines keep trying to introduce other kinds of shoes, with the exception of the ballet slipper, most of the medium heel or other kinds of heels (like wedge heels), have had only a minimal appeal. For the last ten years, women seem to feel that the high heel is the prime fashion feminine heel.

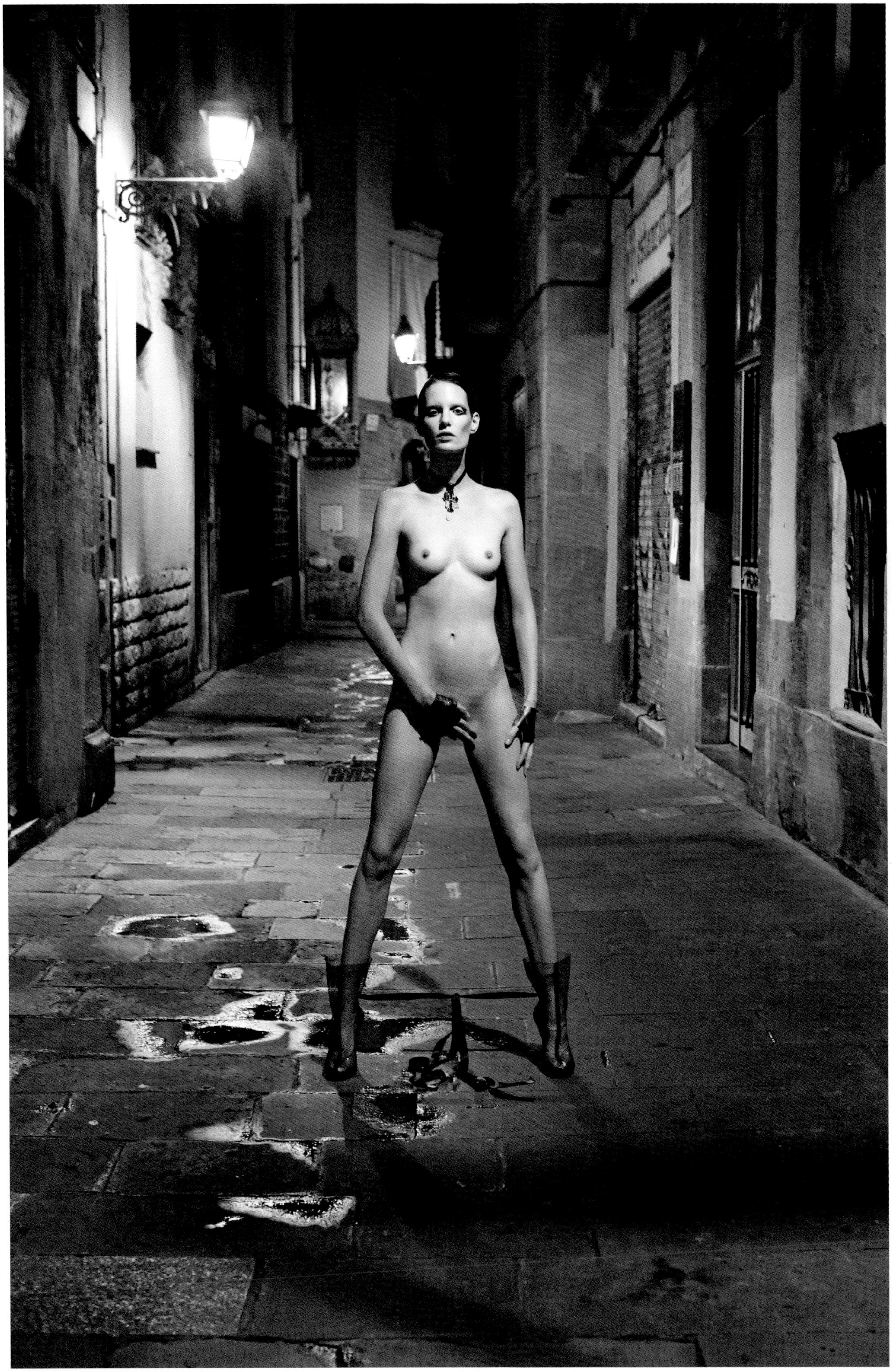

Sebastian Faena, shot for *V Magazine*, 2010.

Why is this the case?
There are a number of different factors. One is that clothing itself has tended to become more uniform. There's a lot more mix-and-match, high and low mixing in clothes too. Nobody wants to look like a fashion victim whose fashion is too extreme. So there's been a kind of dressing down really. There's less of an emphasis on extreme clothing so shoes have become the one part of the wardrobe where there seems to be more room to show off a high fashion quotient and personality. Of course, that feeds into women's interest in shoes and love of shoes. That's one of the main reasons. People have also gotten used to the idea that they could take off their high heels and put on some flats to run and catch the subway and then slip the shoes back on for a glamorous entrance. You certainly see that happening during fashion week. Whether people during fashion week are wearing skinny jeans and a chic sweater, or even if they may be dressed in high fashion, they've almost all got high heels on.

Often you'll see them changing a couple of blocks away. When they're there among their peers—other fashionable women—they want to be wearing high heels because that's the standard of being a fashionable person. Especially now, with the internet and blogging, everybody feels that they can potentially be part of that circle of fashionable women and so high heels have started to seem *de rigueur* for everybody.

In your book Shoes: A Lexicon of Style, *you say that shoes say more about the wearer than almost any other item of apparel.*
That's because there's so much conformity and uniformity in dressing that shoes are the area where you can play and you can show whimsy or fierceness or whatever. But it's hard to say whether you show more personality, because you have one personality. The fact that you have a lot of shoes doesn't mean you have multiple personality disorder. I think it'd probably be more accurate to say that with shoes you can show your attitude and

This spread: Brian Finke. Opposite: *Untitled (Bodybuilding 93)*, 2005.
This page: *Untitled (Bodybuilding 24)*, 2004, from the series "Most Muscular."

feeling for that day. Not just your personality but your persona that you want to present. You can have more multiplicity playing with the shoes.

What do high heels say about the women who wear them? Does it have to do with ideas of status and luxury?
No, because you can get cheap high heels. Plus, it's the context. On Tenth Avenue, wearing high heels might say that you are a hooker. Somewhere else, it might say that you were dressing up because you were going to a date and going out to a fancy restaurant. Somewhere else, it would say that you're a member of the fashion elite. Or, you're an important business executive and you're dressed up to meet a client. It has a combination of meanings, which range from sexual to status indicators.

Shoes in general have changed so dramatically. In the 1970s a high platform with a super high heel in shiny black patent with an ankle straps around it and chains meant you were a dominatrix.

Now all this stuff is just part of the normal characteristics of a lot of high fashion shoes. So it doesn't necessarily indicate a specific sexual significance. It could just mean *these* are fashionable shoes. All that sex has already been packed into fashionable shoes now. Back in the 1970s, a photographer like Helmut Newton would have to go to fetish stores to get super high heels for his photographs. Now they are available everywhere.

Why do you think so many fashion designers have started their own lines of shoes in the last ten to fifteen years?
Money. There's *a lot* of money in shoes. A lot of companies make more money on shoes and handbags than they make on dresses. They're not necessarily cheaper to produce but more people are likely to buy them. You can get more fashion bang for your buck. Even if you're paying, say, $800 for a pair of shoes, the price of a dress these days can be three or four thousand dollars. So you see, you get a lot more fashion bang for your buck.

This spread: Luciana Val & Franco Musso, shot for *10 Magazine*. Styling by Sophia Neophitou.

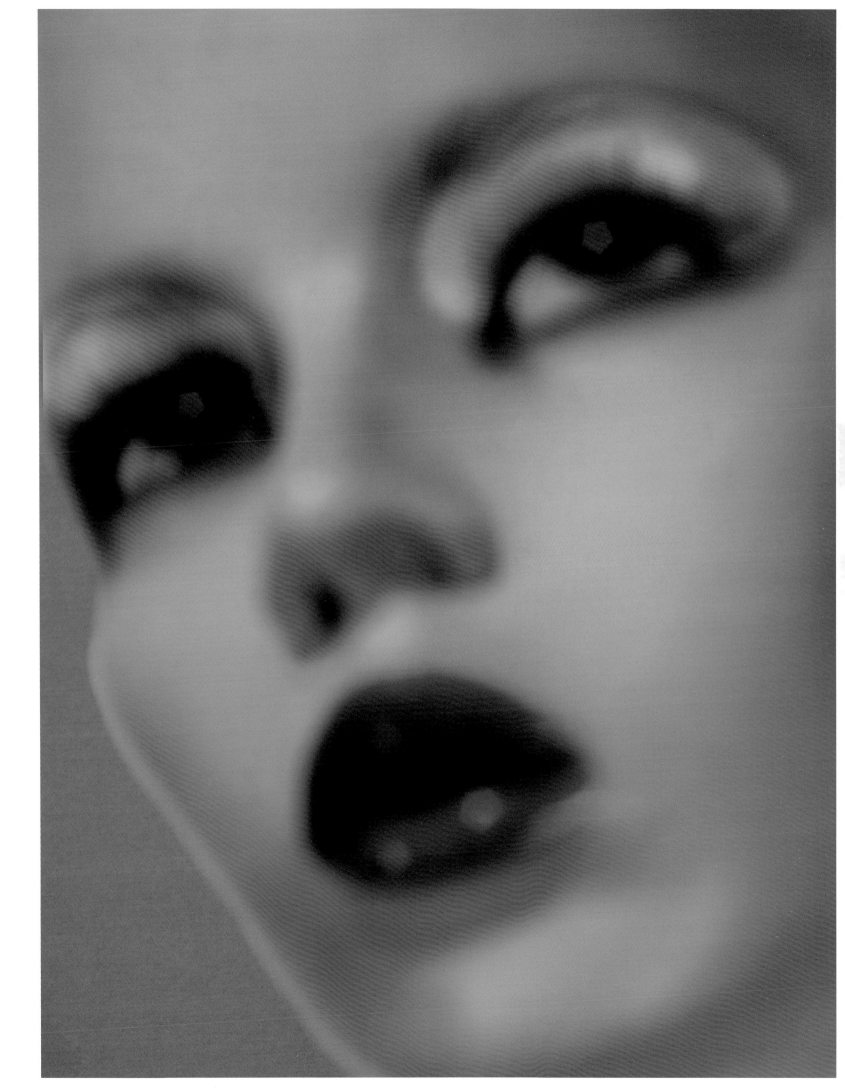

*In tandem with this shift, high heels are becoming more extreme
in terms of height, concept, material, and embellishment. What
do you think is happening here?*

Extreme shoes have become really common on the fashion
runway and, as a result, shoes that a few years ago would have
seemed really high now just seem high but not particularly high.
People will photograph them so you can get press for collections.
Some people will buy them and then they will be photographed
by various paparazzi. If you can walk in them, it makes a pretty
impressive image. And since there's a widespread attraction to
and interest in high heels, if you can do a one-up on somebody
by wearing even higher heels then that's part of the natural infla-
tionary tendency in fashion. It's like crinolines in the nineteenth
century—they got bigger and bigger until they got so big that the
wearer couldn't get through the door. These shoes will keep on
getting as high as they can until they literally can't be walked in,
which is sort of where some of the runway ones are.

Indeed, models do fall down on the runway.

It's a little terrifying watching some of the shows. You're just
cringing watching because the girls—a lot of them—are so
young; they don't really know how to walk in those really extreme
shoes. You've imported a bunch of fifteen-year-old models from
Eastern Europe. They're not necessarily practiced like some old
drag queen.

*What about Alexander McQueen's Armadillo shoes—were they
designed to be worn?*

Oh, yes, absolutely; they were designed to be worn. But not worn
by the masses. You don't want that in fashion anyway. Design
should be an exclusive, striking, distinctive thing—you see a
picture and you know immediately those are the Alexander
McQueen Armadillo shoes. The next step is to have a very high
shoe that has no heel. That's already something that some
designers do. Lady Gaga and Daphne Guinness wear some very
extreme shoes. There's a wonderful Japanese designer, Noritaka

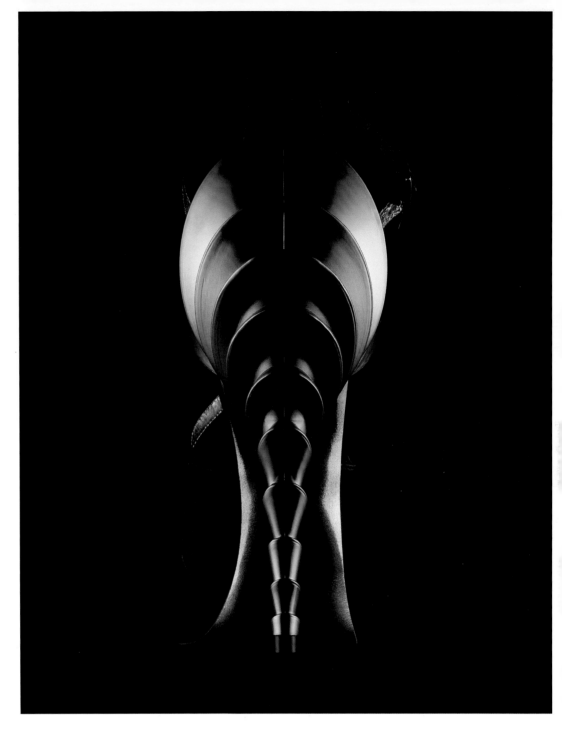

Opposite: Philip Karlberg, *Untitled* from the series "Kasthall," 2008.
Pages 65–67: Koichiro Doi, shot for *Italian Vogue*, 2008.

Tatehana, who's done some amazingly high but heelless shoes. You're just balancing on the ball of your foot. It's a one-upmanship. It's a tremendous engineering feat for the designer. It has to be very carefully calibrated. And then it's quite a bravura performance by the person who's wearing them.

It all tips into the fetish realm with a lot of these extreme heels. The whole iconography of sexual fetishism in general has just been incorporated into the fashion vocabulary and it now just signifies sexy. Severe heels no longer means that someone is a dominatrix. Fashion is a big Hoover vacuum cleaner. It sucks up all kinds of powerful images from anywhere around, whether it's subcultures like sexual subcultures or music subcultures. Once it has taken them in, the meaning changes. Some of it involves open-mindedness but some of it just involves iconography that's been more or less stripped of meaning. It retains only a vague sexual association and doesn't connote a kind of sexual practice. For most people, it's just 'sexy.' They don't look at the ankle straps and think of bondage.

Images of the shoe are consumed as much as the shoe itself. We forget how much people consume fashion through their eyes and not just by wearing it on their bodies. In fact, probably the main way most people consume most fashion is just through their eyes. I remember when I was researching *Shoes*, a lot of people told me that they bought shoes even without really thinking whether they were going to wear them. They bought shoes because they were beautiful objects. They talked about them in terms of sculpture. You could say that they were like images that people wanted to consume and to be able to look at. Maybe part of it has to do with the built-in shape. Most clothes without the body look like an empty skin. Whereas shoes really have a personality and a look to them all by themselves. You could put them on a shelf. Or some people store their shoes on a shelf in the closet so they can see all of them. I'm sitting at my desk and I've got my feet up on my desk and I'm looking at my shoes and I'm thinking, "those *are* a nice pair of shoes."

Interview conducted by Justine Parker.

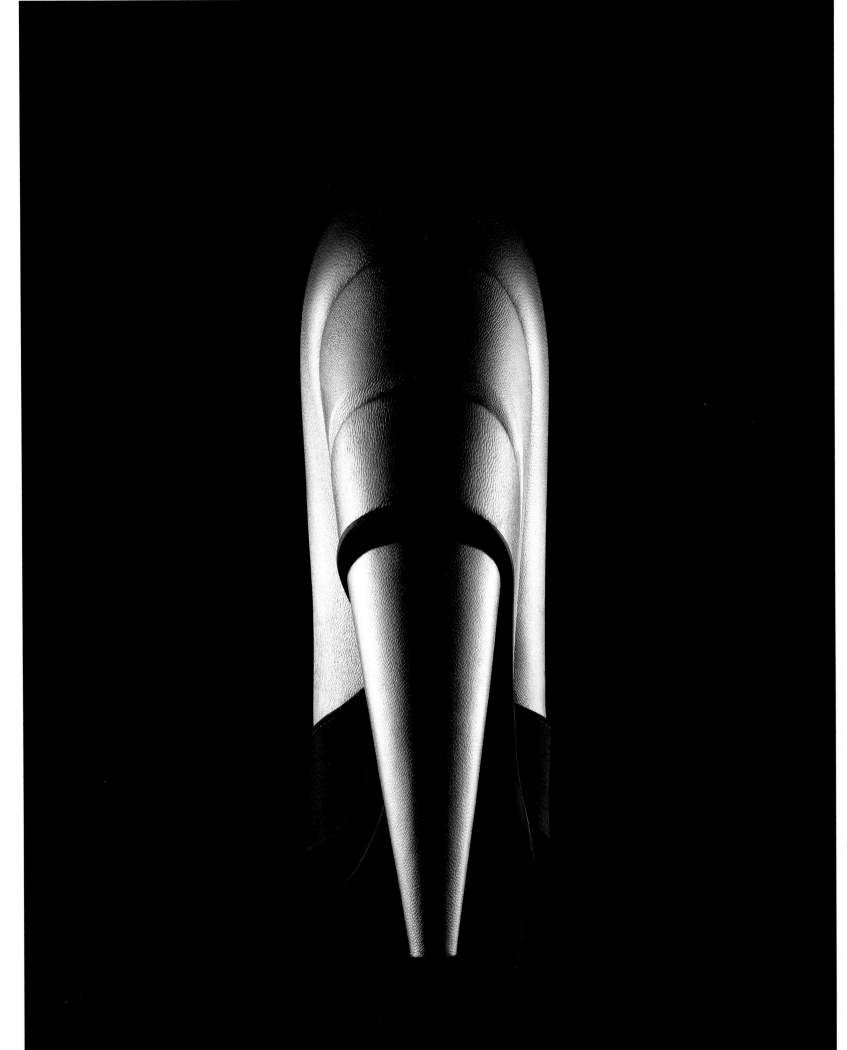

Warren du Preez & Nick Thornton Jones, shot for *i-D Magazine*, 2008.

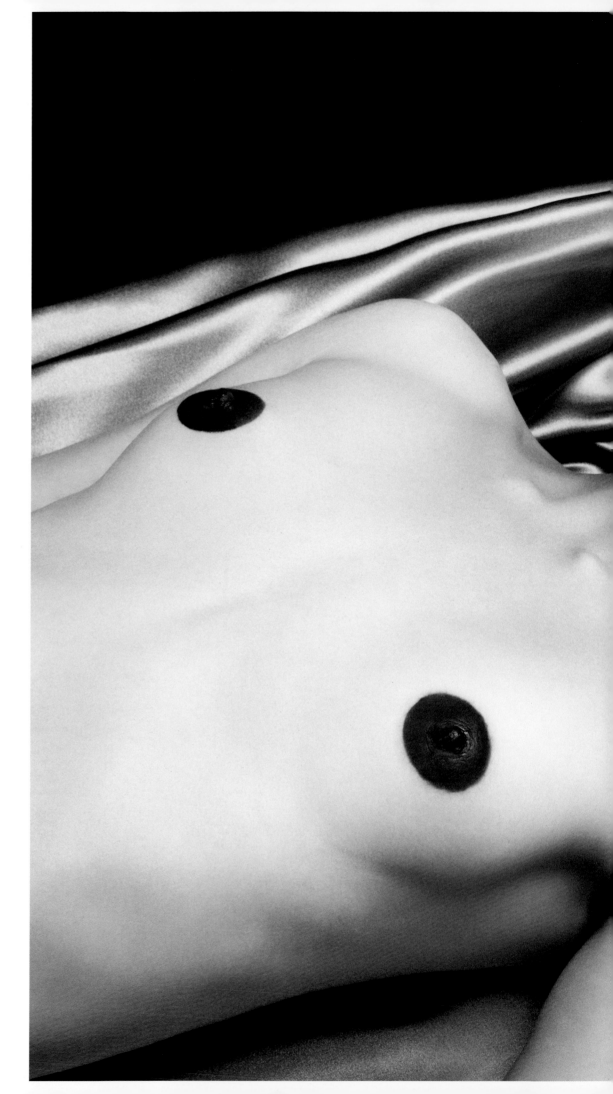

Dusan Reljin, *Stoya*, shot for FW10/SS11 Lipstick issue of *Exhibition* magazine.

Roxanne Lowit, "How to Survive Wedding Season," 2008, for *Marie Claire.*

Opposite: Claudine Doury, *Le camp Kiparisni #2*, from the series "Artek," 2002.
This page: Warren du Preez & Nick Thornton Jones, shot for *Muse Magazine*, 2006.

77

Juergen Teller, *Laura Dern, Paris*, 2007.

This spread: Roxanne Lowit.
This page: *Fran Lebowitz in New York*, 1984. Opposite: Backstage at Viktor & Rolf.

This spread: Michael James O'Brien. This page, top: *Harnais (Felipe), Paris, 2007.* Felipe Pizarro wearing leather arm piece by Rex, Paris. This page, below: *L'envol, Paris, 2007.* Silver shoes by Betony Vernon. Opposite:*Still life with a corset by Mr. Pearl, Paris, 2008.*

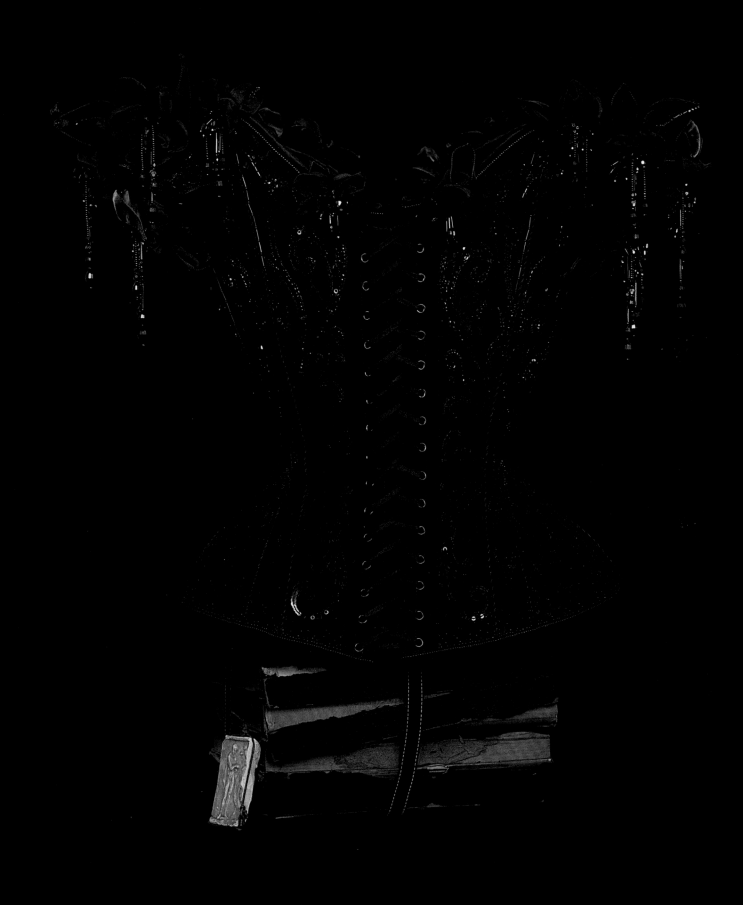

Jeff Burton, *Betony Vernon (Casa Mollino)*, Turin, 2007.

Miles Aldridge, for *New York Times Magazine*, 2007.

Pages 95–97: Rankin. Opposite: From the book *Visually Hungry*, 2007.
Next spread: *Silhouettes*, for *Dazed & Confused*, 2007.

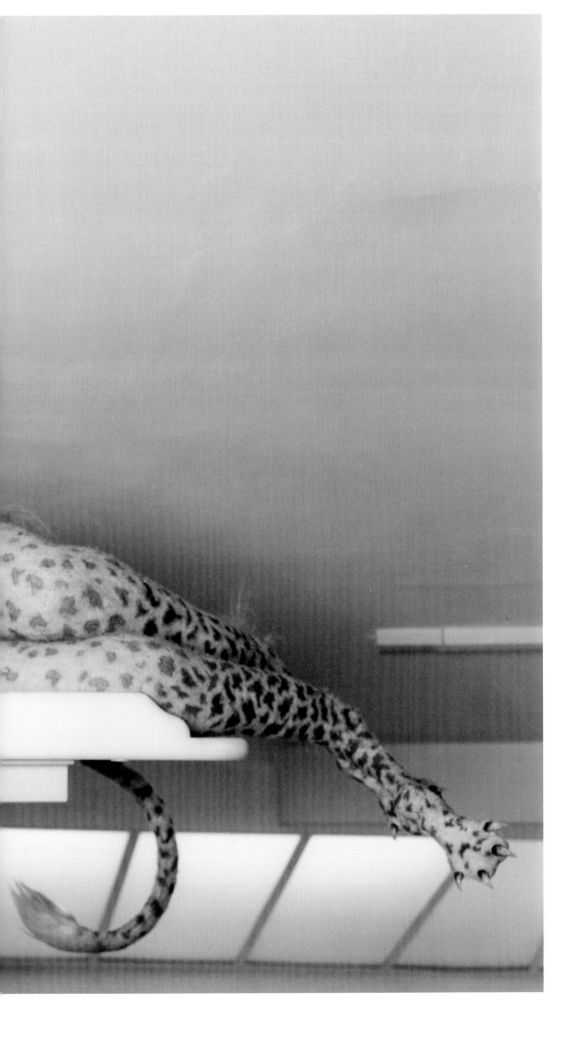

Matthew Barney, Production still from *CREMASTER 3*, 2002 ©2002 Matthew Barney. Photograph by Chris Winget. Courtesy Gladstone Gallery, New York.

Alex Majoli, *Escort Service, New York City*, 2005.

Marcus Bleasdale, *Paris: The finale at Lanvin*, shot for *New York Magazine*, 2009. © Marcus Bleasdale/VII.

Pages 104–106: Shoe designs by Manolo Blahnik, Autumn/Winter 2011–2012.

Tim Blanks

in conversation with

Manolo Blahník

How old were you when the form of the high heel first impressed itself upon you?

I always liked the lower extremities. When I was growing up in the Canary Islands, all the little boys and little girls on the beach, I didn't even look at their faces, I looked at their feet. But I'm not a fetishist, I just loved the feet. I didn't even see it as engineering, they were just very expressive to me. My mother would have all these teas, and the ladies would come, and I was always looking at what they were wearing. And I looked down always, at the leg and this ... *thing* that was planted on your extremity between the heel and the leg. There are pictures of me as a little boy holding shoes, touching shoes, eating up shoes.

What did they look like at that time?

I was very attached to the volume of the mid-1940s heel. It was not really thin, nor was it vulgar or chunky. It was something very stable and beautifully balanced. The stiletto changed the whole thing. The shift in volume from the fat heel to the thin heel was a big shock. It was almost perverse to see that tiny Roger Vivier thing coming out. But things changed aesthetically. Fat heels didn't conform with the aesthetics of people. Still, I believe most women care about comfort. They see life is difficult and in moments of anguish, they need something comfortable. I see a return to that look.

I find the negative space of the high heel fascinating. It's something you convey really well in the pictures you make of your shoes. Each of them seems to be telling a secret.

I do it unconsciously. For me the secret of the shoe is, first, the line, then the balance, then the way a woman walks in them. I even like those monstrosities I see. But now I'm bored. I'm sick of hooker shoes with platforms. I want to return to some kind of normality, to beautifully, solidly made stuff. I was just in Savannah, Georgia and, late at night, I saw *Idiot's Delight* with Norma Shearer and Clark Gable, and the way she moved, the way she showed her ankle... yes, the heels were fabulous at the beginning of the '40s, when Adrian was doing the costumes and Ferragamo was doing these *old bag* shoes... I liked the moments in those black-and-white films when you saw the shoes. I am a child of the movies. We didn't have TV when I was growing up in the Canaries in the '50s. When I think of Barbara Stanwyck in *Double Indemnity*, crossing her legs, with the marabou chain around her ankle... it was the *ankle*!

The power of suggestion was so much stronger then.

I belong to the school of getting inspired by the past. Josephine and the Queen of Naples and Elisabeth of Austria, the ghosts of these women come back to me and say so much because of their rigour and style. Heel-less shoes? Can you imagine the Empress

Elisabeth in the eighteenth century? Or those Latin girls, the 40s divas like Celia Cruz, walking in heel-less shoes? But you actually *see* the heel, because the focal point is not the bloody heel, it's the *curve*.

Is seduction the goal?
I don't see it as seduction, I see it as transformation. I always think of shoes as a theatrical gesture. The high ones imply a different walk. You have to concentrate on your balance. You move differently. You transform yourself in seconds when you put on a high heel. It's great to combine artificiality and everyday life. I think it's got to do with that aura of—how do you say the word?—*inaccessibility*, out of reach.

A fantasy?
No, I don't think it's a fantasy because that's *beyond* out of reach. But "out of reach" is *almost* unapproachable. *That's* the word. I love that. It's to do with my twisted mind, or whatever it is. I adore women, but they're a phenomenon I'll never truly know. Yet when a woman is wearing the shoes, I am totally *her*. I don't think of myself as man or woman or anything.

That's testament to the extraordinary intimacy of what you do. It's easy to see why shoes always get linked to sex.
I've never been interested in that. I've totally abolished it. But maybe it manifests itself in other actions in life. Maybe my shoes are the communication I have with people. Maybe they're the act itself. I guess so, subconsciously.

In the interests of empathy, have you tried heels yourself?
I once went to a party at Porchester Hall where I was told to wear a suit and heels. It was *hell* for me.

Well, given the foot, a high heel is a strange, unfunctional object.
Sometimes, I think, oh my god, it's not natural, it's perverse. And the visual perversion of it *is* divine. But when you do it beautifully—get the stand, the *balance* right—it becomes natural. For instance, I have friends who cannot walk in flats. Of course, flats are the most difficult, the most *sensuous* thing.

Tim Blanks

in conversation with

Nicholas Kirkwood

What is the signature Nicholas Kirkwood heel?
It's constantly evolving but it's probably a high heel on some type of internal platform. It has a very distinct silhouette of tapered shapes with a mixture of round and sharp edges while emphasizing the heel. I used to have obvious platforms but I'm trying to get away from that. It's about sitting down and having an idea— coming up with a shape.

The high heel is a cliché. People think of them in very reductive terms. As a shoe designer do you think the high heel is the ultimate creative challenge?
There are two schools of designers. Either you evolve your aesthetic or you start by reinventing a complete concept. The latter happens more in ladies wear, like with Marc Jacobs—who's revolution. I'm the evolution-type. Someone like Chanel or Manolo Blahník use their recognizable styles. You can identify their designs from the other side of the room. I hope the same is true for my shoes. There's a look to it, whether it evolves each season or not. There are six or seven constructions every season and every structure gets redone almost every time. You can't do everything completely new new but you can at least strive. Evolve it.

That's interesting because that's the way things move forward. There's a proposition, the thesis, the antithesis, and there's the synthesis where the height and the practicality combine. The foot is a finite proposition.
It's finite but at the same time you can look at it like it's a blank canvas. In some ways, there's an infinite amount that can be done with the shoe. The restrictions being that the foot needs to go in and shoes be worn.

Is there a point where a heel crosses over into fetish?
That's always something I've really tried to avoid. High heels don't necessarily have to be so sexy. It's also the shape or the style rather than just only trying to be sexy.

Do you think there's a sort or sexiness in the implication of incapacitation?
I think there is. On the other hand, you can also work that. In other words, by making a women higher—making her stand tall—she can be empowered. Even just being that little bit higher can be a source of transformative self-confidence. You can look at it as putting women on a platform—on a pedestal.

Pages 107–109:
Shoe designs by Nicholas Kirkwood, Autumn/Winter 2011.

At what point does it stop being realistic?
When girls are falling over in the shows. There was a point where every other show girls were falling over because designers were pushing it too far. I'm even responsible for some of that too. That's where it kind of became a joke. Those kinds of shoes belong in a museum rather than being worn.

I think the way a high heel holds a foot is also very much the way a bra holds the breasts.
Exactly. How's a guy going to know that? I have to take people's word for it. You just have to take the best average of what people tell you. Obviously every foot is different. Different parts of the world have different shaped feet as well, separate to everybody within those regions also having different feet anyway. So it's very difficult. You've got to come up with your best average and just do it that way.

Do you think for women generally there's an idea of restraint and self-awareness in women's clothing that doesn't exist in men's clothing? The whole point of bespoke tailoring for men is that you just put it on and you don't think about it anymore.

Whereas the opposite is true for women's clothes.
I think the feminine now is far less restrained. Maybe they're just restrained by how much it costs. It's all about social status. Now it's about intellectual superiority in being able to distinguish different makes and seasons. That's the interesting thing about fashion. It's not going all in one way. Not everything is getting more casual. Some heels are becoming more and more restrictive and more difficult to walk in. Maybe we'll go back to corsets being very tight.

Restrictive or not, at the very least extremity is more common. How does that translate into what you do? Do you feel you have the opportunity to be more extreme now?
It's more acceptable to be more creative but being so extreme—by just trying to make the highest heel—seems passé and uninteresting. If you look at Venetian Chopines, some of them were two feet high. In the past there's been so much extreme footwear, far more than even today. There's still so much to explore without extreme heights. Extreme shoes don't have to be high, for example.

How liberating is technology for you?
Technology allows you to do many new things and ever newer technologies become available all the time. 3D printing used to be an impossibility. There are certain types of machine cutting that are so intricate that it can no longer be done by hand. One thing that I would love to invent—but I'd need to go to NASA—is something to replace Velcro. I hate the way it looks but I love what it does—invisible fastening. There has to be a way and I want to come up with that eventually. That's my mission for the next twenty years. In the past, the invention of plastic molded heels, for example, has allowed us to do so many things that weren't possible. You'd never be able to do a high and skinny heel in the 1800s. Heels have got a plastic spike down the middle. I know it isn't romantic—no little Giuseppe filing away a wooden heel—but probably at least since the 1970s, high heels are injected plastic molding. You can make them out of wood but they just snap.

Did that totally change shoe design, having the plastic injected?
Right at the beginning, it probably didn't. People were sort of stuck into the broadly accepted way shoes should look. So initially people didn't really experiment with it. Since then, it has allowed us to do so much more.

Could there be something else that changes shoes as radically as injection molding? What could it be?
I think it's like 'what else could there be' and when everybody says 'everything's been done before.' It hasn't. You could put something on your foot that makes it disappear because it's made of a fabric that's used on stealth tanks. That hasn't been done with shoes yet. So I want to do that, so it looks like you're floating above the ground.

Tim Blanks

in conversation with

Charlotte Olympia

The balance of a woman's body is so different from a man's, which is what you're taking into consideration when you're making a shoe.
Can men ever really understand the physical sensation of a high heel? I mean, they can't. Trying it out for one night is one thing, but you're not living it. In a way, women practice wearing high heeled shoes their whole lives, adapting to it. I grew up wearing high heels, trying on my mother's shoes when I was little. So I don't know how a man does it—if they do it just purely aesthetically. But as a woman, you just know. You can feel the slightest thing when it comes to a shoe, even down to the millimeter. That's how technical it is. Salvatore Ferragamo was technical about it—or as technical as a man can be. He truly studied the science of it. As a woman, though, you try them on and you know. You feel it.

Would you say you started designing shoes to make shoes for yourself?
Initially, I guess so. I never grew up saying I wanted to design shoes. I wanted to be in fashion design. But then, as I grew up, I got more involved in corsetry and lingerie and supportive constructions in

particular. When I did my foundation course at the London College of Fashion, one of my teachers told me to make shoes. After I made my first pair, I realized it was something I could get used to doing. I then went to Cordwainers Technical College.

How did you find that? How useful was that for you?
It's quite necessary to understand your trade somewhat. You have to understand how to make what you're designing rather than just drawing, especially when it's such a technical craft. Plus, I work more in three dimensions anyway. I like to work three dimensionally to the last. Though I sketch the shoes myself I'll never draw magnificent illustrations like Manolo does.

It's interesting that you came out of lingerie and corsetry into shoes. There are real codes to lingerie, to corsetry, and to shoes. There are definite rules, which gives them such a link.
Quite a link! Apart from them being completely feminine and what women love and spend their money on the most—underwear and shoes—there is a link. They're quite structured, restricted, sexual.

Do you think then that what you do is a sort of art? Is it an exercise in sculpture?

Shoes are something I like to look at. They're beautiful and even though I might not ever wear them, I don't put them in a cupboard. It's a shame to put things like that away. For sure, I think shoes are sculptural. I like them to look as good off a foot as they do on. I like all the lines to be ergonomically worked into every little detail. Even the inside of the shoe. The sole of the shoe. Everything. Maybe because that's what I do with shoes. I look at them. Before I made my own, I used to have a little book case that was glass fronted. I put all my favorite shoes in there. I've got a few from Gucci, like the bamboo-heeled ones. Some Yves St. Laurent ones—all crystal! The super high Giambattista Valli ones, which were the only shoes I wore before I started making my own because they were the highest out there. Super high! Now I look at some of the shoes that I thought were high and they're not *that* high.

High heels are the one item that are completely for women. But women haven't really been designing them until now. Why do you think there are now more women designing shoes?

For a start, there are quite a few more women doing everything in general. I have always wondered why don't women design shoes. We're the ones that wear them. It's the same with clothes too. It's puzzling. Maybe they just like to see them and collect them.

You have to do something which is going to seduce women, and something that is special. At the same time, wearers are more aware how a shoe is made, which propels designers to incorporate the latest technology. It's a combination of the necessity of shoes with the demands for the very latest technology that gives a shoe its lightness and durability. Something that interests me about shoes—and hats, for that matter—is the suggestion of a sort of negative space. Sometimes it's not just what you're looking at; it's what around what you're looking at.

Exactly. That's what I was saying about liking shoes that look as good off as they look on. It is the negative space in between the heel and the platform that can look too weird and wide or it can be perfect. The lines make the spaces inside, outside, and around the shoe.

111

This page: Sylvie Fleury. Above: *Diptyque*, 2008, cast bronze, gold patina and chrome. Courtesy of the artist. Below: *Video stills from Bells*, 2003. Courtesy of the artist. Opposite: Val and Franco. Shot for *El País*, 2010. Styling by Sebastian Kaufmann.

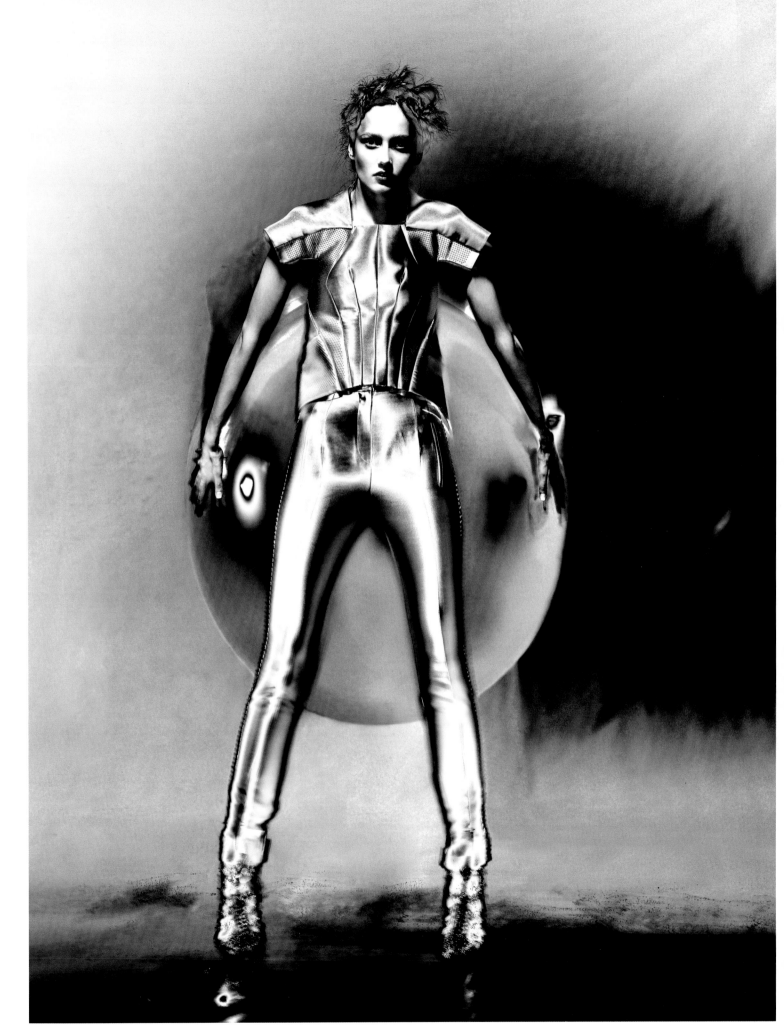

Opposite: Toby McFarlan Pond, for *Liberation Next Magazine*, 2007.
This page: Warren du Preez & Nick Thornton Jones, shot for *Muse Magazine*, 2008.

This page: Barrie Hullegie. *Untitled*, 2010.
Opposite: Luciana Val & Franco Musso. Shot for *Numéro*, 2009.

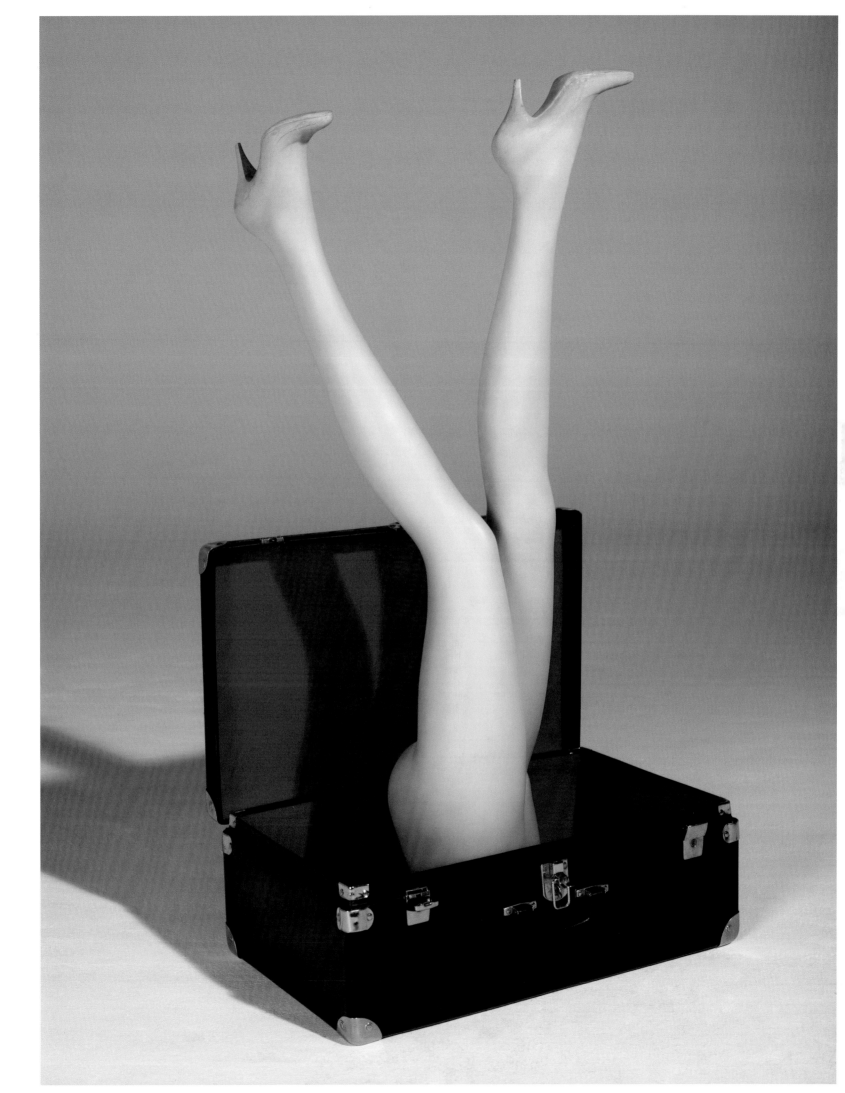

Sean and Seng, shot for *Numéro*, 2011.

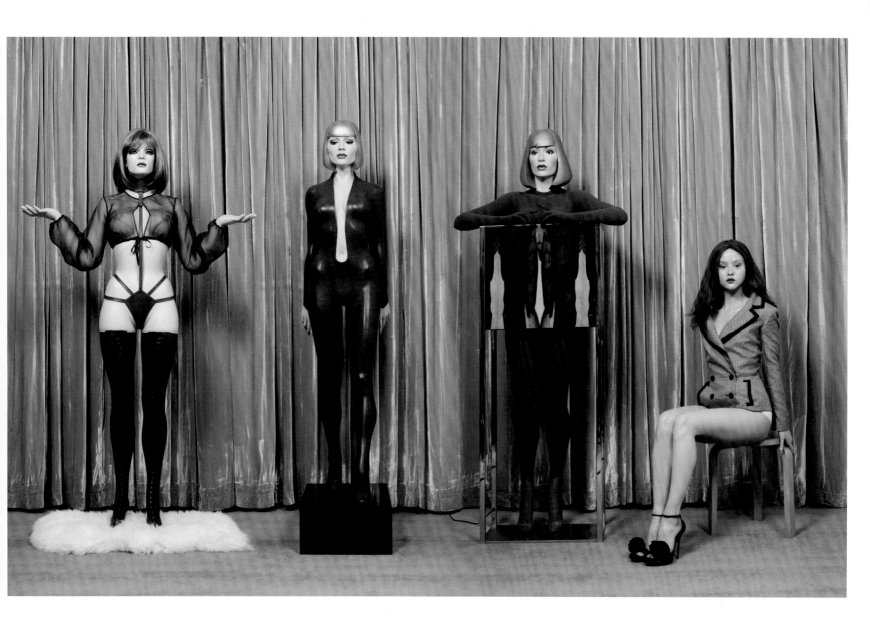

This spread: Sean and Seng, *Untitled* from the series "Wearable Art," published in *Pop Magazine* 2010.

This spread: Glen Luchford, *Poster Child*, shot for *V Magazine*, 2010.

Pages 124–129: Marilyn Minter. This page: *Splish Splash*, 2005. Opposite: *Stepping Up*, 2005. Pages 126–127: *Swell*, 2010. Page 128: *Runs*, 2005. Page 129: *Streak*, 2010. All images courtesy of the artist and Salon 94, New York.

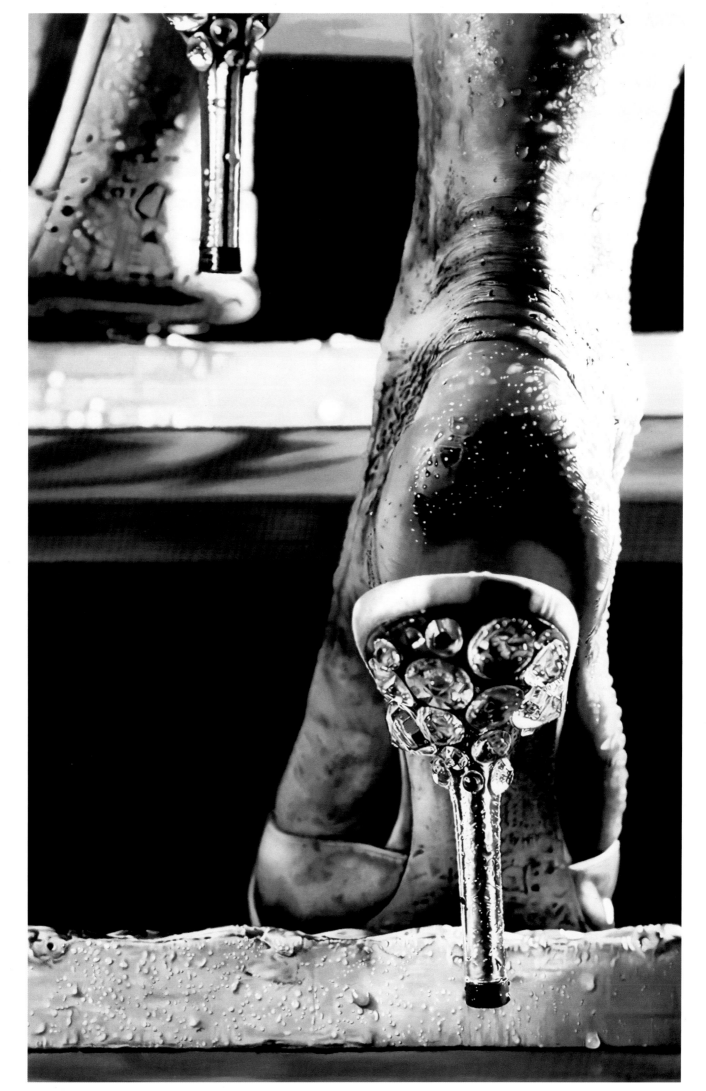

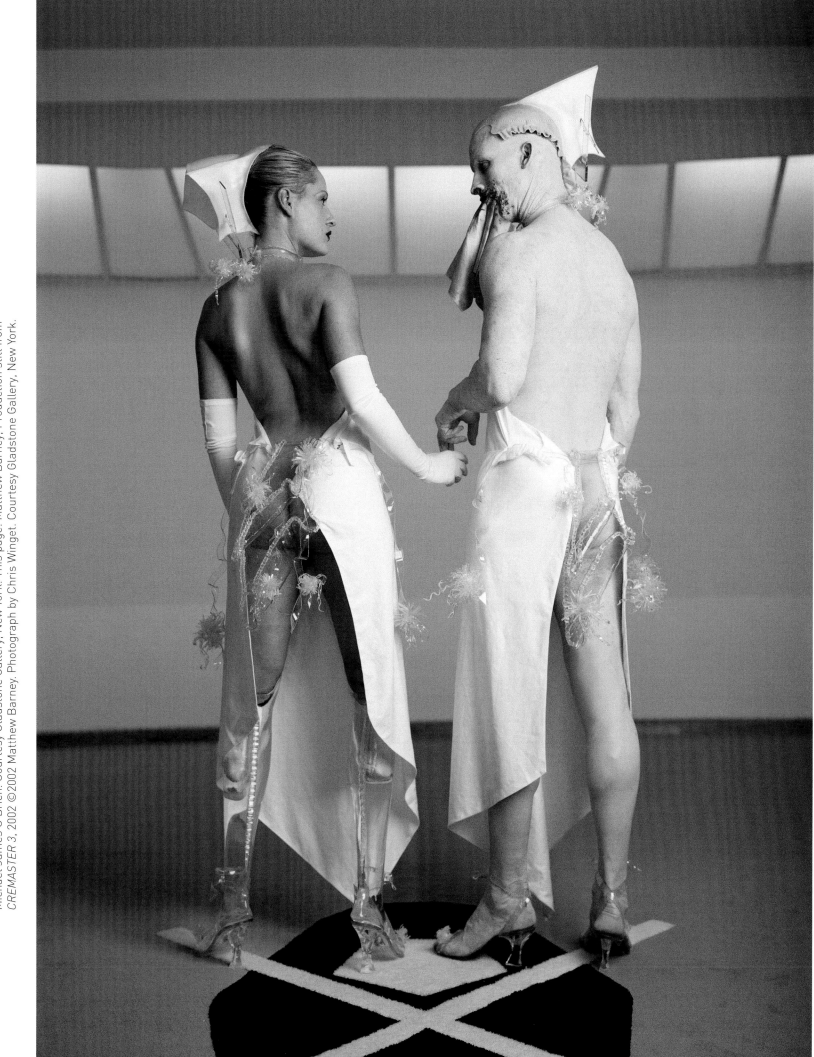

Opposite: Matthew Barney. Production still from *Drawing Restraint 7*, 1993 © 1993 Matthew Barney. Photograph by Michael James O'Brien. Courtesy Gladstone Gallery, New York. This page: Matthew Barney, Production still from *CREMASTER 3*, 2002 ©2002 Matthew Barney. Photograph by Chris Winget. Courtesy Gladstone Gallery, New York.

Pages 132–135: Lise Sarfati. This spread: *Christy #01*, from the series "Austin, Texas," 2008. Next spread: *Jennifer #01*, from the series "Austin, Texas," 2008.

Larry Sultan, *Boxers, Mission Hills*, 1999, from the series "The Valley," 2001.
Courtesy the Estate of Larry Sultan and Stephen Wirtz Gallery, San Francisco.

Larry Sultan, *Sharon Wild*, 2001 from the series "The Valley," 2001. Courtesy the Estate of Larry Sultan and Stephen Wirtz Gallery, San Francisco.

Pages 141–143: Tim Walker. Pages 141–142: shot for *Italian Vogue*, 2008.
Page 143: shot for Hermès Catalog, 2009.

This spread: Sølve Sundsbø. Opposite: shot for Numéro, 2004. This page: shot for Numéro, 2002.

This page: Craig McDean, shot for *W Magazine*, 2006. Opposite: Walter Pfeiffer, from the book *Cherchez La Femme*.

Above: Barrie Hullegie, *Untitled*, 2010. Opposite: Warren du Preez & Nick Thornton Jones, shot for Cartier, 2002.

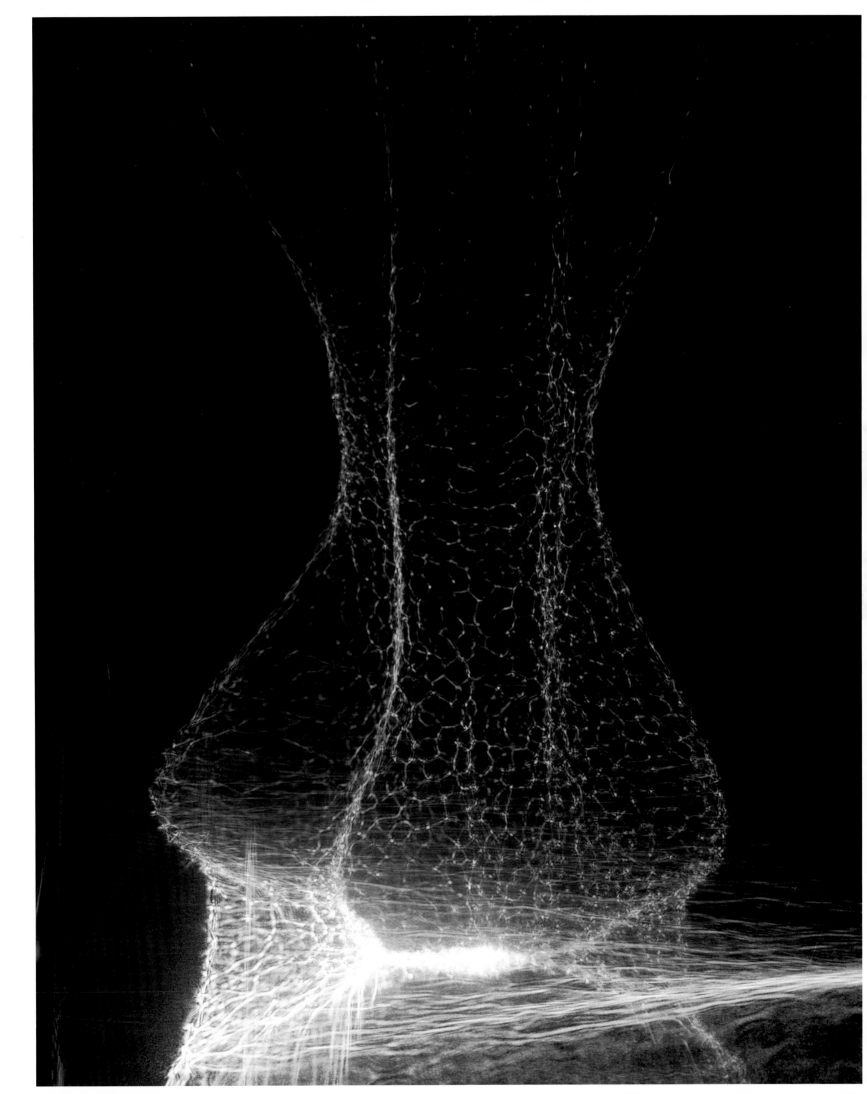

This spread: Barrie Hullegie. *Untitled*. 2010.

Miles Aldridge, *Kristen*, for *Paradis Magazine*, 2009.

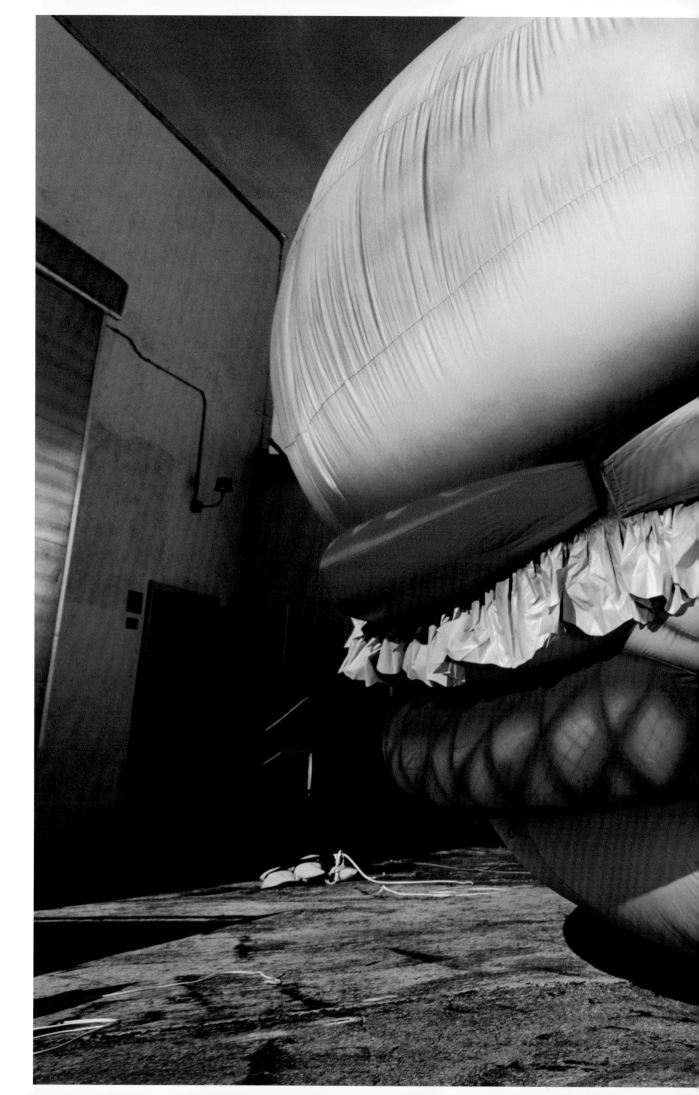

David LaChapelle, *Death by Cheeseburger*, shot for *Vogue Italy*, 2002.

David LaChapelle, shot for *Vogue Italy*, 2002.

This spread: Wendelien Daan, Alek Wek shot for *Citizen K*, 1999.

This page: Martin Parr, Clare College May Ball, Cambridge, 2005.
Opposite: Peter Marlow, Felix Naylor Marlow in Fiona's high heels
watched by his brother Theo Naylor Marlow, 2005.

This page: Jeff Burton, *Corina [peep-toe shoes]*, 2006.
Opposite: Anuschka Blommers/Niels Schumm, 2002.

Jeff Burton. *Untitled #36 (poolside w/silver pumps)*, 1995, from the monograph *jeff burton / untitled*, 1998.

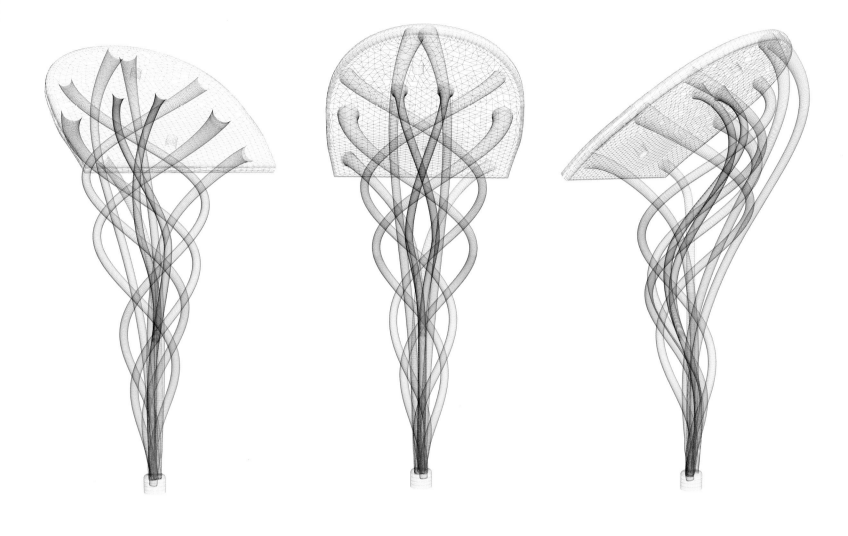

Techno Heels

by Philip Delamore

Creating couture is about showing the extremes of technique in materials, construction and decoration—technology in its purest sense, as it relates to the skill and craft of the couturier and the artisans who collaborate to create each item. Today this application of technology includes new digital, computer-controlled tools and machines for creating shoes that have become increasingly extreme and unique.

The idea of convergence of technologies from different disciplines, such as architecture, automotive and product design is central to the digital revolution that is driving the new aesthetics and production of shoes. No longer simple court shoes with stiletto heels—increasingly adventurous feet are adorned in techno-sculptures, autoerotic furniture for the feet.

As we increasingly delve into the connected world of the internet, our various online identities are becoming multiple avatars of our possible selves, immortalized on the web. So we are also beginning to express more facets of our selves in the real world, and what we wear, especially shoes, offers a pantheon of possibilities for remodelling our bodies and expressing our alter-egos.

In the last decade there has been a huge shift in the landscape of design and manufacturing, enabled by 3D design, new prototyping and manufacturing processes, and new materials. As shoes can be considered closer to hard products than clothing, they have caught the attention of product designers and architects who were the first to explore these new computer aided design tools and who could apply them to much more readily commercial products, than the few and far between large building projects for which they were ultimately designed.

Once the preserve of large firms with pockets deep enough to invest in AutoCAD systems, the last decade has also seen the democratization of these design tools, as both computer processing power increased and cost decreased (in accordance with Moore's law), and the improved graphics cards in home computers driven by the games and film industries allowed for much better quality viewing. This meant that a new vanguard

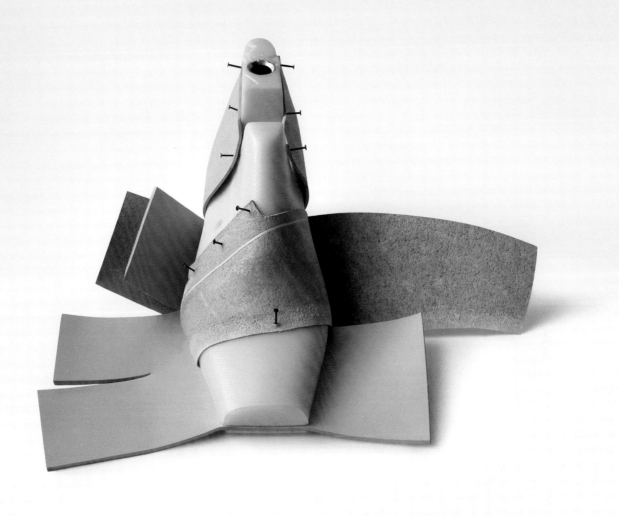

of designers has emerged who are able to develop their skills and implement new approaches to design using inexpensive and readily available software.

At the same time, much of the traditional manufacturing of shoes, which had been done in Europe, has moved to new hi-tech manufacturing plants in China and the far east, where factories are better equipped and more willing to experiment with new production processes, and materials.

Young designers graduating from universities are now more likely to embrace these new techniques and materials because they allow them to have more control of the process, while the complexities of components and assembly are now far removed from their geographical reach and pocket. In the same way that traditional craftsmen of the medieval guilds developed their own tools in the workshop to enable them to more efficiently form, shape, and join the materials at their disposal, this new generation of hacker-artisans are creating software tools and 3D-printed components, or drawing on more readily available production processes from other industries.

The creator of the modern stiletto heel, Roger Vivier, introduced a metal rod into the heel in the 1950s to give strength and stability to the slim and vertiginous heels. His legacy is now given a twenty-first century revision by designer Kerrie Luft, whose first collection uses a 3D laser sculpted heel of titanium metal. The process called direct metal laser sintering is usually used to produce medical implants and aerospace parts from 3D CAD models, but in this case forms an elegant twisting matrix which is extremely light and very strong (page 166). The heels are created from a metal powder that is melted by lasers scanning across the surface and building the shape layer by layer. This technique allows designers the freedom to create new forms that would be impossible to make with traditional casting or moulding processes.

The concept behind the United Nude brand is that it is an international collective, and an example of the move towards convergence in design, and a more conceptual approach to

169

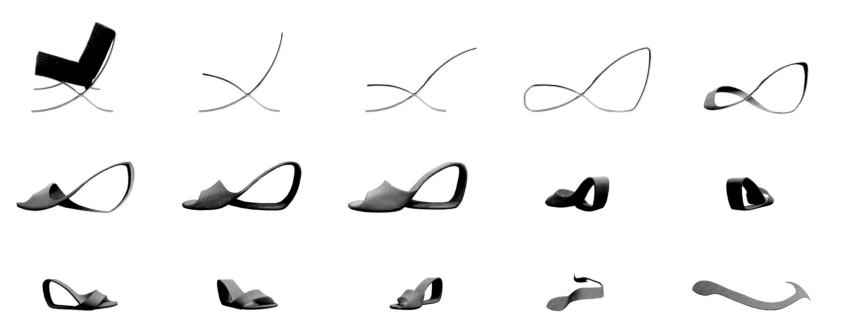

footwear (page 167–169). Co-founders Galahad Clark, from a very British footwear family, and Rem D. Koolhaas from a well known Dutch architectural background, launched the UN brand with the Möbius shoe in 2003 (pages 169 below, 170). The shoe is a series of sinuous curves inspired by Mies van der Rohe's Barcelona Chair, and the principle of the Möbius strip, which took one hundred prototypes and two years to get to market, "No one that knew about shoe manufacturing would attempt the Möbius because they appreciate how complicated something like this is to produce," says Galahad. The design has endured, and a new Ultra Möbius has just been launched using carbon fibre components and new moulding techniques, which were developed for the shells of luxury yachts and Formula One cars.

Another UN concept, the Lo-Res shoe was developed with a software company to allow the designs to be created through a 3D editing process (page 169 above). The triangulated facets of the shoe reflect the digital aesthetics of the "polygon mesh"—the new building block of the digital and architectural world around us, the

glass Kryptonite structures rising out of city centres around the world by architects such as Zaha Hadid and Norman Foster.

This idea of building a series of iconic products around design concepts, rather than following fashions seasonal contradictions is shared by a number of young shoe designers.

Marloes ten Bhömer studied product design in Arnhem before her footwear Masters at the Royal College of Art. She finds the shoe a fascinating object to design: "it has to do with identity and fashion but practically it has to be worn, and be structurally sound in motion. As opposed to a chair, a shoe is more about the wearer and identity, I also thought it was a skill I could take on, something I could practically do."

There is a tension between the craft and the machine made, especially when the traditional associations of bespoke and couture are with the poetry of the hand, and the hours of work put into every piece in small ateliers and workshops. Marloes suggests that the luxury products we currently fetishize are in fact just as likely to be made in a large factory, as in small workshops, and that perhaps it

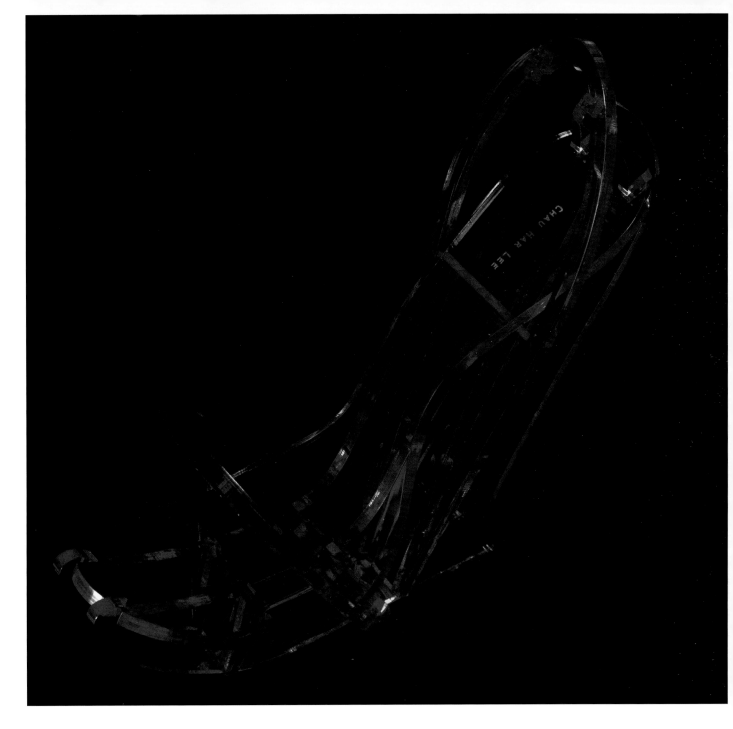

is more about how new digital tools may enable the small independent makers to flourish." To me using digital tools is much more about the possibility of producing small quantities and experiments with shapes, constructions and the possibility to produce something outside the set regimented production of footwear."

Chau Har Lee shares the approach of "design as research." Although trained in traditional footwear design at Cordwainers, Chau was later exposed to 3D scanning and design software used in architecture and car design (pages 171–173). Working from a scan of her last she began to experiment with 3D prototyping, as she found the complexity of traditional process could be overcome by quickly 3D printing her concepts: "traditional shoe making is a beautiful craft, but it is frustrating if you can't make to the standard and quantity required. New technology allows you to explore how the two come together—it ultimately brings a new aesthetic as you are approaching it from a different direction." She also points out that "if you look at shoes through history there are no real rules as to what a shoe should look like."

With this in mind Chau begins by trying to forget what is out there and "do something from scratch, to strip a shoe down to its essential functions of support, and what materials would suit a heel in order to bear the body's weight." Using a variety of techniques including laser cutting, 3D printing and welding she creates concept pieces which then can be made into more wearable styles. Like the UN Mobius, one concept has been under development for three years, working with materials developers to create the perfect balance between design and materials.

Current research at the London College of Fashion is taking this approach even further to analyse the way people walk in heels by using arrays of sensors fitted into shoes, to better understand how the forces are exerted on the foot in motion, and how this may be applied to designing shoes in the future.

So consider then, how much underlying science and technology may be embedded in the objects of desire which adorn your feet, next time you pull on a pair of heels.

Noritaka Tatehana, Coral, 2010.

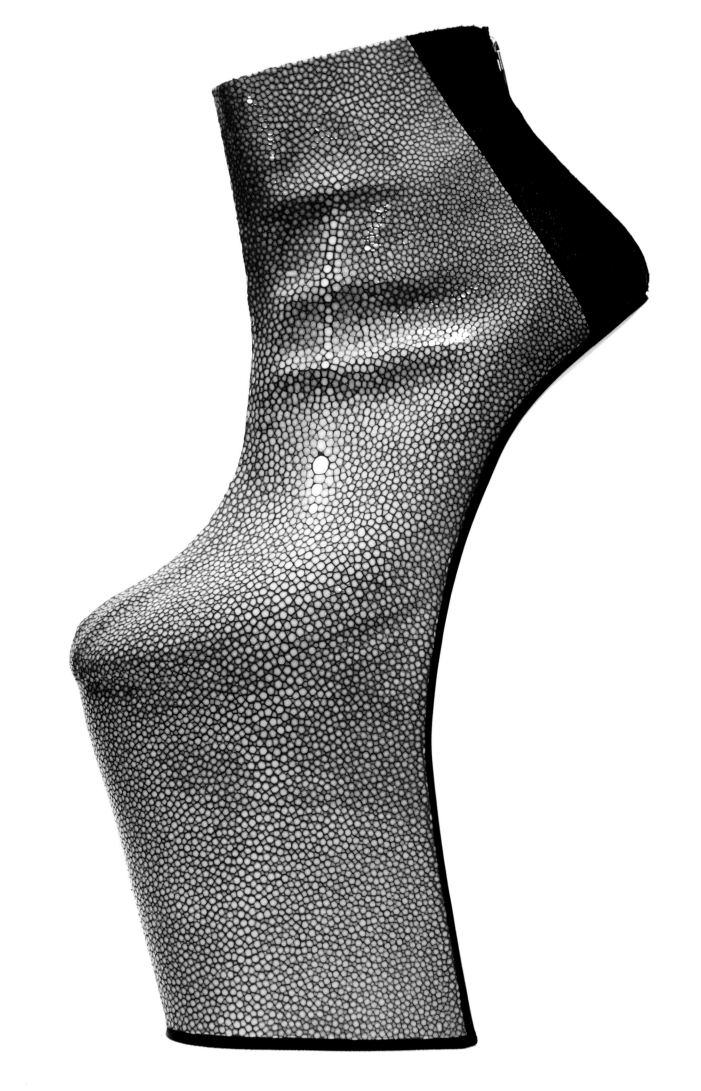

Alexander McQueen, Armadillo Shoe, 2010.

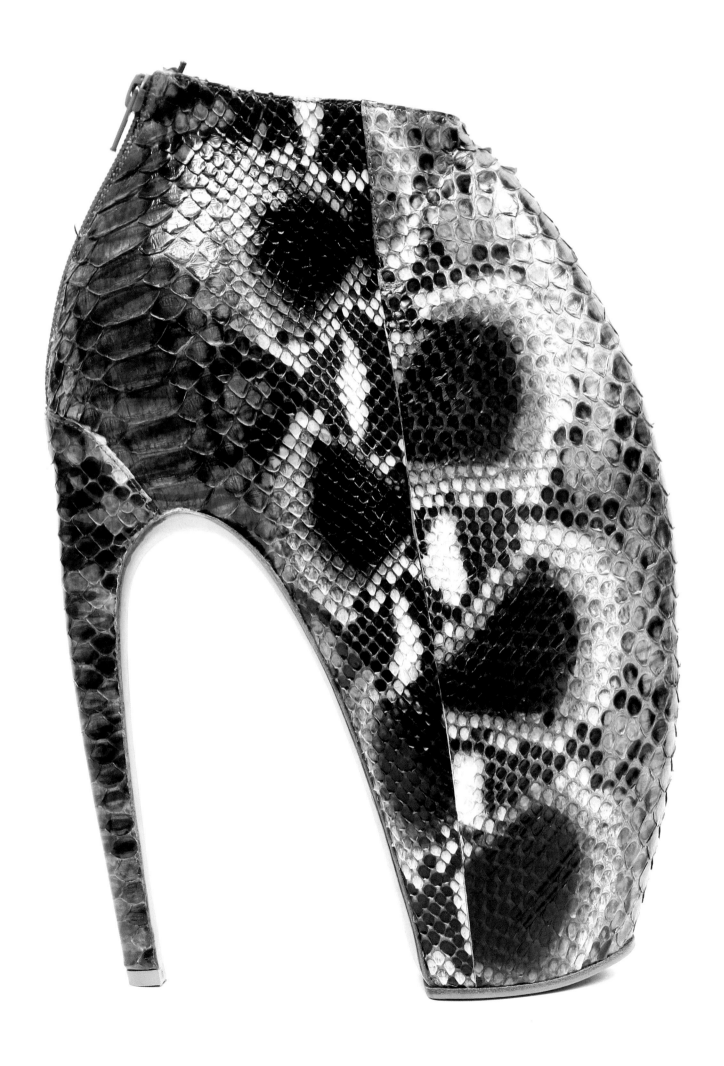

Opposite: Alexander McQueen, Alien Shoe, 2010. This page: Walter Pfeiffer, shot for *I-D Magazine*, 2009.

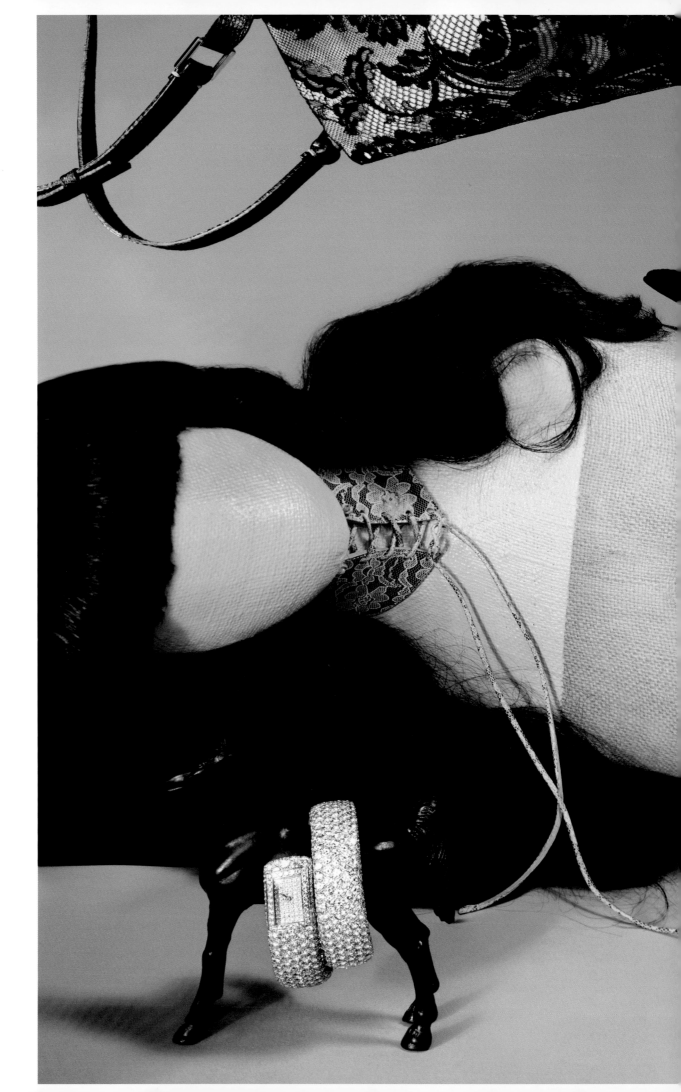

Craig McDean, shot for *Harper's Bazaar*, 2000.

Heels on Screen

by Stella Bruzzi

High heels are innately dramatic; couple this with the fact that they are one of the most persistently important signifiers of femininity, and they become the ultimate cinema costume accessory. High heels readily represent different feminine archetypes, from the domestic, to the fashionable, to the dangerous, seductive feminine such as the *femme fatale*. Frequently—but certainly not exclusively—high heels enhance a female character's glamorous appeal. Studies of film costume (especially women's costumes) often alight on the symbolic value of clothes: that, as feminist film scholar Jane Gaines has articulated, costumes tell the woman's story. High heels can, in this way, be flexible signifiers, depending on the characters they adorn and the outfits they complement. The *femme fatale*'s sharp weapon-like heels borrow the accoutrements of the fetish parlour, but equally, the housewife of 1950s Hollywood melodramas wears the high heels of conformity and conventionality and Grace Kelly the delicate footwear of Dior's New Look mannequins.

Many films use heels—particularly when coupled with sharp toes—to increase a female character's dramatic impact; think, for example, of Sharon Stone in the most infamous scene of Paul Verhoeven's thriller *Basic Instinct* (1992). Brought in for questioning in a murder inquiry by hapless Michael Douglas, Stone—at the height of her powers as a modern day Hollywood temptress—has changed into a pristine white outfit of short fitted dress, loose coat and stilettos. During her questioning by five cops (drably attired in functional grey suits), Stone discards her coat and, facing the men, crosses and uncrosses her legs. The sequence is notorious for Stone's lack of underwear, its drama accentuated by the pointed pale shoes that hover, sometimes tantalisingly out of shot, at the end of her extended tanned legs. High heels are the *femme fatale*'s ultimate weapon; not only do they accentuate her femininity by elongating her legs, but they are literally weapon-like. In *Basic Instinct* Stone's shoes recall specifically the ice pick used as the murder weapon.

The dangerous woman's fetishistic appeal is explicitly signalled again in John Dahl's 1990s' noir *The Last Seduction*, in which Linda Fiorentino plays the *femme fatale* who escapes the law dressed for the most part in short black skirt, stockings and high heels: part office worker, part dominatrix. Conversely, in many of the 1940s noirs the connotations of the *femme fatale*'s dress code are more ironic, her intentions more closeted: Barbara Stanwyck in blocky white heels descending the stairs at the start of *Double Indemnity* (Billy Wilder, 1944) or Lana Turner in white peep-toe sandals in Tay Garnett's 1946 version of *The Postman Always Rings Twice* that complement the summer ensemble of white turban, cropped top and shorts she wears to ensnare John Garfield are not so overt embodiments of evil womanhood.

The double association with criminal seduction is the most straightforward way in which the drama of high heels has been adopted by film. Although on the publicity poster one of Victoria Abril's black stilettos has a smoking gun for a heel, in Pedro Almodovar's early comedy *High Heels/Tacones lejanos* (1991), high heels remind Abril of her mother coming home when she was little. High heels can also connote fragility, an over-reliance on appearance and masquerade. A key classical example of this is Alfred Hitchcock's *Marnie* (1964) in which Tippi Hedren plays a habitual kleptomaniac, psychologically ruined by repressing memories of having, as a child, killed one of her prostitute mother's clients. The film opens with a dark-haired woman in a plain dark suit and a decidedly obtrusive custard yellow bag nestling under one arm walking away from camera, her heels clicking as they trip along a train platform. We next see her repacking suitcases, switching identity cards and washing black dye out of her hair, eventually returning to her 'natural' identity and state as a peroxide blonde. As she hides away her old clothes in a railway locker, she drops the key on the ground and pushes it through a grate with the toe of her grey court shoes.

Pages 182–185: Sebastian Faena, film stills from *La Mujer Rota*, 2007.

A less dramatic and potentially unanticipated use of high heels is as an accessory to traditional, domestic femininity, for instance in melodramas. Self-consciously citing the 1950s melodramas of Douglas Sirk and Vincente Minnelli, in which Jane Wyman or Deborah Kerr played unhappy or unfulfilled middle-aged women bound to their home and domestic maternal duties, Todd Haynes' *Far From Heaven* (2002) uses the hyperbolic, exaggerated costumes by Sandy Powell as metonyms for Julianne Moore's frustrated state. Haynes' homage to the golden age of melodrama offers an ironic commentary on the entrapment of 1950s' middle-class American womanhood, with its women adopting, more or less willingly, the era's uniform of ballooning skirts in rich, bold colours, matching accessories and dainty feminine court shoes—too high to be functional, too conventional to be erotic.

Functionalism and eroticism are binary opposites and so, usually, are functionalism and fashionableness. The functionalism of high heels is, in films, often brought into question: Grace Kelly discarding her taller heels for loafers in *Rear Window* (1954); Audrey Hepburn wearing pumps rather than heels when relaxing in *Funny Face* (1957). Alongside the suppression of their ultra feminine footwear what we see in these examples is the twinned suppression of the women's own erotic potential. The two are so often synonymous as in *Modesty Blaise* (1966) when Monica Vitti teeters in her elegantly fashionable or in *A View to a Kill* (1985) as Grace Jones becomes the comic monster in her shiny black vertiginous heels.

When it comes to being fashionable, however, high heeled shoes are not always essential accoutrements, although it has become more so with the recent success of couture-centred films such as *Sex and the City* (2008) and *Sex and the City 2* (2010) or *The Devil Wears Prada* (2006). In an earlier film such as Luis Bunuel's *Belle de jour* (1967), Catherine Deneuve as the high-class part-time prostitute wears an exclusive mid-1960s Yves Saint Laurent capsule wardrobe, rounded off by a set of patent leather, buckled

low-heeled court shoes. Here, the combination of fashion and fetishism produces a demure appearance as opposed to the declamatory fetishistic look of Jane Fonda in *Barbarella* (1968). The *Sex and the City* cycle has brought the fetishistic potential of high heels back into cinema, most prominently through Sarah Jessica Parker's endorsement of first Manolo Blahník and subsequently Christian Louboutin. The actress's over-identification with spectacular, scene-stealing footwear reached such a height before the release of *Sex and the City 2* that the internet gossip magazine 3AM Gossip Tonic mused about Parker: "Ah, Sarah Jessica Parker running in inappropriate shoes, how we've missed you." The accompanying image was of Parker publicising *SATC2* in mid-2010 wearing $1,000 McQueen Oil Backzip sandals and various other vertiginous heels. Parker's high heels became, over the years, the series' ultimate fetish objects and the Louboutins she wears in *SATC2* are so outrageously ostentatious, so clearly selected because they knock your eye

out that, as shoes, they have far transcended their function as accessories to round off an elegant feminine ensemble. Whereas I began by citing various ways in which heels were symbolically reflective of a woman's character, by the time we get to *SATC*, the women's characters are subservient to, if not directly defined by what they wear. Costume is found to be no longer slavishly subservient to identity and character, so Sarah Jessica Parker's high heels are objects of eroticism and desire as enduring as Parker herself.

Opposite: Trent Parke, *An office worker disappears into the shadows of a building on Pitt Street*, from the series "Dream/Life," 1998. This page: Elliott Erwitt, *New York City*, 1978.

Pages 188–191: Antoine D'Agata. This spread: *Stygma Lithuania, Vilnius*, 2004.
Following spread: *Private Club Artemis, Germany*, 2006

Authors and Acknowledgments

Ivan Vartanian is an author and editor based in Tokyo, Japan. His publications include *ArtWork: Seeing Inside the Creative Process* (2011), *Setting Sun: Writings by Japanese Photographers* (2007), and *Japanese Photobooks of the 1960s & 70s* (2009), which was the recipient of the 2010 Historical Photobook award at the Arles International Festival of Photography. In 2011, Vartanian's imprint Goliga will pubish *Accident*, a photobook by Daido Moriyama.

James Crump is Chief Curator and Curator of Photography at the Cincinnati Art Museum. His published works include *Variety: Photographs by Nan Goldin* (2009), *Albert Watson* (2007), and most recently, the revisionist monograph, *Walker Evans: Decade by Decade* (2010), named one of the top ten books of the year by *Library Journal*. In 2007, Crump wrote, produced and directed the acclaimed documentary film, *Black White + Gray*, featuring the influential curator and collector, Sam Wagstaff and artist, Robert Mapplethorpe.

Valerie Steele is Director and Chief Curator of The Museum at the Fashion Institute of Technology. She has curated more than twenty exhibitions, including *Gothic: Dark Glamour*; *Love & War: The Weaponized Woman*; *The Corset: Fashioning the Body*; *London Fashion*; and *Femme Fatale: Fashion in Fin-de-Siècle Paris*. She is also editor-in-chief of *Fashion Theory: The Journal of Dress, Body & Culture*, which she founded in 1997. Steele is also the author of numerous books, including *Gothic: Dark Glamour*; *The Corset: A Cultural History*; *Paris Fashion*; *Fifty Years of Fashion: New Look to Now*; and *Fetish: Fashion, Sex and Power*. She was editor-in-chief of the three-volume *Encyclopedia of Clothing and Fashion*.

Tim Blanks has been covering fashion for more than twenty years, first as host of the internationally syndicated television series *Fashion File*, now as editor-at-large for Style.com. He writes regularly for *Vogue*, *GQ* and *Interview*. He has also contributed to a number of books, most recently the catalogue that accompanied the exhibition *Alexander McQueen: Savage Beauty* at The Metropolitan Museum of Art, New York, and Walter Van Beirendonck's new monograph.

Philip Delamore is a Senior Research Fellow in Digital Technologies, and the Director of the Fashion Digital Studio at the London College of Fashion, University of the Arts London. Delamore brings twenty years of experience in the fashion industry to his specialist field of research, which is in the convergence of fashion design and technology, regularly collaborating with experts in the fields of human, material and computer sciences to develop new approaches to design thinking and practice. He has recently exhibited work in Milan, London, and Stockholm, and is currently developing new research in the field of Digital Fashion.

Stella Bruzzi is Professor of Film and Television Studies at the University of Warwick, UK. Among her many publications are several on fashion and costume, including *Undressing Cinema: Clothing and Identity in the Movies* (1997) and the co-edited *Fashion Cultures: Theories, Explorations and Analysis*, to come out in a second edition in 2012.

The preparation of this volume was made possible by the efforts of many individuals, who graciously contributed their time and encouragement. In particular, the editor would like to extend his thanks to the following individuals: Tim Blanks, James Crump, Valerie Steele, Stella Bruzzi, and Philip Delamore for their insightful contributions; Justine Parker, Tiffany Godoy, and Loren Fykes; Lesley A. Martin and Melissa Harris of Aperture Foundation; Jason Evans, Penny Martin, and Kyoko Wada; Jamie Camplin, Natalie Evans, Aaron Hayden, Rowena Stanyer, Maria Blessing, Alison Rutherford, and Jaime Tung of Thames & Hudson, Ltd.; Todd Bradway, Elisa Leshowitz, and Luke P. Brown of Distributed Art Publishers/D.A.P.; Elisa Uematsu and the staff of Taka Ishii Gallery, Tokyo; Kozue Yamada of Angle Management; Myles Ashby of Art + Commerce; Justin Stuart Rose of Trunk Archive; Karin Lund and Sandra Tysk of LundLund; Jordan Shipenberg of Art Department; Jonathan Bell and Junko Ogawa of Magnum Photos; Cat Celebrezze and the Peter Hujar Archive; The Estate of Antonio Lopez; Catherine Johnson-Roehr of The Kinsey Institute for Research in Sex, Gender, and Reproduction; Daphne Guinness; Carmen Scott of Creative Exchange Agency; Manolo Blahník, Nicholas Kirkwood, and Charlotte Olympia; Chau Har Lee; Chenelle Hall; Axel Sourisseau of Agence Vu; Ella Toal-Gangar; Nick Papadopoulos of VII Photo; Etheleen Staley; Thomas Brannigan; The Robert Mapplethorpe Foundation; The Estate of Guy Bourdin; Sascha Crasnow of the Gladstone Gallery, New York; Philip Tan of the Matthew Marks Gallery, New York.

First published in the United Kingdom in 2011 by Thames & Hudson Ltd, 181A High Holborn, London WC1V 7QX

British Library Cataloguing-in-Publication Data
A catalogue record for this book is available from the British Library

ISBN: 978-0-500-51572-3

Printed and bound in Singapore

To find out about all our publications, please visit **www.thamesandhudson.com**. There you can subscribe to our e-newsletter, browse or download our current catalogue, and buy any titles that are in print.